3,001
ARABIAN
DAYS

3,001
ARABIAN
DAYS

Growing up in an American
oil camp in Saudi Arabia
(1953-1962)
A Memoir

RICK SNEDEKER

STATION
SQUARE
≡ MEDIA ≡
NEW YORK, NEW YORK

PRAISE FOR
3,001 ARABIAN DAYS

"I thoroughly enjoyed this involving and enchanting period book about Arabia and America in (mostly) more innocent times of the '50s and early '60s. This memoir of mid-century life in Saudi Arabia, with all the weighty issues of oil, social taboos, expatriates, Wahhabism—plus Little League baseball—is documented here in a disarmingly humane, affectionate, and insightful manner by a son and kid brother who got it all first-hand over the Kingdom's and his own formative years."

— PETER THEROUX, AUTHOR OF "SANDSTORM: DAYS AND NIGHTS IN ARABIA" (1991) AND "TRANSLATING L.A." (1995)

"*3,001 Arabian Days* has everything a reader wants in a book, with a congenial narrator to lead you on an adventure in an exotic locale and in a lost era. While the book will be of special interest to those with a connection to the Arab world or to the oil business or ARAMCO, I had none of those and yet found myself charmed by the author's effortless storyteller's style. It is a book that is both an escape and an education."

— DALE DAUTEN, ENTREPRENEUR AND AUTHOR OF "THE GIFTED BOSS" AND "THE MAX STRATEGY."

"Author Snedeker's wit and insights illuminate the book's easy narrative. His journalistic style faithfully recreates the people, places and events, and keeps the story crisp and moving from one chapter to the next. More than a coming of age story, *3,001 Arabian Days* is a moving tribute to the intricacies of family, a celebration of Saudi Arabian culture, and a glimpse into a time gone by, but whose shadowy specter you can still almost reach out and touch."

— MARK KENNEDY, SAUDI ARAMCO WRITER/EDITOR, DHAHRAN

"… a heartwarming and informative book, laced with lots of humor …"

— BILL "BEANIE" MANDIS, TEACHER, WRITER, MUSICIAN AND
ARAMCO BRAT

"Rick Snedeker lived a 'Leave It to Beaver' childhood but with the distinction of having been transplanted to Saudi Arabia. He documents it here with a remarkable head for detail and a whole lot of affection."

— PAUL SAUSER, FORMER DHAHRAN-BASED EDITOR OF SAUDI
ARAMCO'S ARABIAN SUN, THE COMPANY NEWSPAPER FOR EMPLOYEES
AND THEIR FAMILIES.

"Rick Snedeker is a keen observer, an engaging storyteller, and a gifted writer. In *3,001 Arabian Days*, he brings his talents to tales from the early days of Aramco and Saudi Arabia. After several decades of sweeping economic and social development, that world has disappeared—but Snedeker's pen vividly captures people and places from days gone by. His portraits of family and friends, daily events and life's key milestones, and even the local flora and fauna in Dhahran are all keenly drawn with equal measures of wit, empathy and humor. His recollections are further brought to life by a treasure trove of rare photos drawn from company archives and his own family photo albums. Rick's 3,001 days in Arabia seem to have provided him with a more or less equal number of stories to relate: some wry and funny, some poignant, all insightful."

— GREG NOAKES, U.S.-BASED SAUDI ARAMCO WRITER/EDITOR

"Most Americans have no idea what went on in Saudi Arabia to build the unprecedented oil-production colossus that helped fuel the economies of the post-World War II era. The '50s and '60s were a unique time in Saudi Arabia's history, when the Kingdom teamed with Americans and other Westerners to build the world's greatest energy company— what is now called Saudi Aramco. Rick Snedeker was an eyewitness to this early collaboration. Growing up in Saudi Arabia in those days was a unique blend of typical American childhood adventures and rich cross-cultural experiences that stay with you for a lifetime. Rick tells this amazing story with a journalist's skill, coupled with wit, irony and personal insight."

"To get an accurate understanding of Saudi Arabia today, it's useful to delve into what life was like in the Kingdom in the 1950s and '60s when Aramco was helping to build a modern and thriving country. Rick Snedeker has come as close as anyone to capturing the magic of growing up as an American "Aramco brat" in Saudi Arabia, doing so in a personal and touching manner that anyone who remembers their own childhood can likely relate to."

3,001 Arabian Days:
Growing up in an American oil camp in Saudi Arabia (1953-1962), A Memoir

Copyright © 2018 by Rick Snedeker
Published by Station Square Media

Editor and Production Director: Janet Spencer King, SK Author Services
Cover/Interior Design: Steve Plummer, SP Design

Printed in the United States of American for Worldwide Distribution
ISBN: 978-1-7322395-0-0

Electronic Editions
MOBI: 978-1-7322395-1-7
EPUB: 978-1-7322395-2-4

ACKNOWLEDGEMENTS

"**B**OOKS AREN'T WRITTEN, they're rewritten," the great medical-thriller novelist Michael Crichton once said, paraphrasing someone else. The aphorism was true when first uttered and holds true today.

That is why my first and most heartfelt acknowledgement is a low bow to my enormously skilled and gracious editor, Janet Spencer King, of New York City. My memoir would have remained lost in a dark, tangled forest of word chaos without her able guidance during and after the arduous but rewarding process of writing and rewriting. And more rewriting. And more rewriting still. But, eventually, purposefully, methodically, she gently led me to the proverbial sunlit glade. She also guided me surely through the self-publishing process until my memoir popped miraculously into view on Amazon and elsewhere. My gratitude is blinding.

I also learned from Janet that publishing even worthy books in a traditional way via a traditional brick-and-mortar, hard-copy publisher is rapidly becoming (if not already there) an avenue mainly useful only to writers who are already famous and beloved by legions of followers. Which, I blush to admit, isn't me—yet. I have thus arrived at the brave, semi-new world of self-publishing, which I discovered is as egalitarian and level-fielded as Facebook and Twitter (at least *before* the Russian hacking of the American election in 2016 perhaps changes everything).

I originally found Janet in a very useful book for budding writers, *Jeff Herman's Guide to Book Publishers, Editors & Literary Agents*, where my indoctrination into the book-publishing industry—and my literary humbling—began. Another very insightful primer for any aspiring writer in today's publishing world is David Gaughran's buoyant *Let's Get Digital: How to Self-Publish and Why You Should*. If knowledge isn't always power, it's always *empowering*. And enriching.

I should note that the manuscript I originally presented to Janet was far better than it had been before my *first* editor, Katherine Turok of quaint-sounding Penobscot, Maine, took it in hand. I also found Katherine in Jeff Herman's book. Katherine ably helped smooth my uneven prose and better organize the nascent book's underlying structure. I am indebted to her.

Many thanks also to my friend and former Saudi Aramco colleague Ted Brockish, who—while on vacation—closely proofread chapters on the company for accuracy.

I also received feedback, historical quotes and nostalgic encouragement from Bill "Beanie" Mandis, an old boyhood pal from my neighborhood when growing up in Dhahran, Saudi Arabia. A few of the charming little girls (now adults) that I had crushes on in my youth kindly allowed me to violate their privacy in my memoir. Much obliged.

For proper photo attributions, I received guidance from Dick Doughty, editor of *Saudi Aramco World*, the venerable flagship cultural magazine published by the Saudi Arabian Oil Co. (Saudi Aramco), and from Todd Williams, editor of the *Arabian Sun*, the company's weekly community newspaper.

An important resource for this memoir was a pristine collection of Dhahran Senior Staff School yearbooks from the 1950s and '60s, that my older brother has kept for many, many years. Just thumbing through the pages provided a warm nostalgic glow, and they also imparted correct name spellings for former classmates and a visual check for accuracy of certain remembrances, such as the layout of the school. Thanks, bro. My dad's extensive photo collection from Arabia was, posthumously, also an enormously useful resource, as well.

But, first and foremost, I want to thank my wife, Pat Aylward, for generously providing the peace of mind and quiet space essential for me in the arduous, preoccupied, solitary process of writing over, literally, years. Without her loving support and renewing companionship, I probably would have quit the project long ago.

My sister, Kathy, provided some real ballast to a generally idyllic youth. Her near-death experience battling encephalitis as a young girl in Dhahran grounded my memoir in reality.

In the end, though, my late parents—Al and Betty Snedeker— deserve the most fundamental kudos. Without their willingness to leave everything behind for an unknown future in the Saudi Arabian desert in 1953, with three young kids in tow, I would have had a far more pedestrian life. And the thought to write a memoir might never have occurred to me.

RICK SNEDEKER
APRIL 12, 2018

To my wife, Pat Aylward, the light of my life.

TABLE OF CONTENTS

Boys of Dhahran, 1950s. (Courtesy Saudi Aramco)

PREFACE

I'M 65 AS I write this and have lived 26 of those years in three distinct periods in Saudi Arabia—literally "Saud's Arabia," named for its founding king with a very long name, Abdulaziz ibn Abdul Rahman ibn Faisal ibn Turki ibn Abdullah ibn Muhammad Al Saud.

In the West, he became known simply as Ibn Saud.

SAUD OF ARABIA

King Ibn Saud's sprawling desert Kingdom had been a sovereign nation for barely 21 years when I first arrived in 1953 as a 3-year-old.

About a fifth the size of the United States, the arid country is the birthplace of Islam's founding prophet, Muhammad, and home to the faith's two holiest places, the cities of Makkah, the prophet's birthplace, and Medina, where he developed and consolidated Islam in exile after being driven from his home town. Initially, Muhammad was a prophet without honor in his own land. But, as we've seen, that changed.

The country also contains the 250,000-square-mile *Rub' al-Khali*—the Empty Quarter—the world's largest contiguous sand desert, where maximum summer temperatures *average* 117° Fahrenheit, and absolute highs can soar to 124°. The endless wasteland has a bit of a Bermuda Triangle vibe. British author and explorer Wilfred Thesiger, who traversed the *Rub'* twice in the 1940s while traveling with nomadic Bedouin, wrote in 1959 that, in separate incidents, an entire *bedu* raiding party and a flock of sheep disappeared in quicksand in the desert's deadly Umm al-Samim region.

BOYHOOD IN THE DESERT

I grew up in the Kingdom from 1953-1962, age three to eleven, when my dad worked there for the then-fledgling Arabian American Oil Co., better known by its acronym, Aramco. We lived in Aramco's initially spartan but cozy east-coast headquarters town, Dhahran—Aramcons referred to it as "the camp"—located about four miles inland from the Persian Gulf (which the Kingdom today officially refers to as the Arabian Gulf) amid a jumble of sandstone hillocks called *jebels*.

Mostly American oilmen and their dependents lived within Dhahran's gated, sheltering confines; Saudi employees and those of other nationalities primarily lived in "Saudi Camp" outside the main Dhahran residential area or in the nearby Saudi towns of Dammam and al-Khobar. The closest such town was al-Khobar, a tiny, dusty, gulf fishing village in the 1950s, now a crowded city.

GOING 'HOME' AGAIN

In 1982 at the age of thirty-two, nine years after picking up a journalism degree at Arizona State University and twenty years since I'd left Dhahran, a friend showed me a fateful classified ad in *Editor and Publisher*, a journalism trade journal. The ad sought a business reporter for a new English-language daily newspaper in Saudi Arabia, the *Saudi Gazette*, based in the West-coast port city of Jeddah on the Red Sea. Ready for an adventure,

I quickly accepted, and shortly thereafter I arrived in boiling, steamy Jeddah.

Luck serendipitously intervened: The *Gazette* arbitrarily reassigned me in July to cover business and general news in the Eastern Province, which meant I had to transfer cross-country to al-Khobar. After a scorching eighteen-hour drive with another reporter in a cranky, AC-free Volkswagen Passat, I found myself several miles from my boyhood home. But it wasn't all nostalgic reverie. My new, *Gazette*-furnished abode was in a shabby five-story apartment block overlooking what was coincidentally named Dhahran Street.

In the years since my youth, the Dhahran-to-Khobar main drag had transformed into a broad four-lane thoroughfare verdant with trees. In my childhood it had been a narrow two-lane blacktop slicing through a trackless wasteland.

Coincidentally, my apartment was only several miles from a non-descript patch of ground on the coast where decades later a sprawling apartment complex would be built—Khobar Towers. Years later, in 1996, jihadist terrorists detonated a devastating truck bomb (packed with more than twenty thousand pounds of TNT) at the complex, killing nineteen American military servicemen bivouacked there and wounding five hundred other victims.

While working in al-Khobar during 1982-1985, I often traveled to Dhahran snooping for news. Astonishingly, I discovered several of my boyhood friends still living there, including several Bills (a popular boy's name in the *American Graffiti* and *Happy Days* milieu of my youth)— Bill "Beanie" Mandis, Bill Scott and Bill Cohea—plus Dave Collier. After graduating from college, the Bills and Dave had returned to the Kingdom to work for Aramco, as I learned quite a few "Aramco brats" had.

My Dhahran reunions in the early eighties with old Little League and neighborhood buddies produced a curious, occasionally disconcerting sense of *déjà vu*. Over the years since, I also randomly and briefly recon-nected in person or online with a number of other Aramco brats from my childhood, including, classmates and muses, Linda Handschin and Chris Reed, Beanie Mandis' sister Kathy, former neighbors Jim and Chery Congleton and Saudi Fadia Basrawi (whose dad was an on-air personality for Aramco TV), and a classmate of my brother's, Suda Prohaska.

LOVE IN RIYADH

In 1985, I left the *Gazette* and al-Khobar to join a New York-based public-affairs company, Burson-Marsteller, as its Saudi-based account supervisor with then nascent Saudi Basic Industries Corp. (SABIC). At that time SABIC was a new government petrochemicals conglomerate based in the Saudi capital, Riyadh, a sprawling boomtown city about four hours west by car in the country's parched, desolate interior.

At a party in Riyadh, I met my future wife, Pat Aylward, a dental assistant from South Dakota then working at King Faisal Specialist Hospital. I returned to the States in 1989, Pat a few months earlier. We ended up together in Vermillion, South Dakota, at the eastern end of the state near the Iowa border, where Pat, a native, qualified for in-state tuition to pursue a degree in dental hygiene at the University of South Dakota. While she learned the art of teeth cleaning in Vermillion, I found a job at the far western end of the state as a copy editor and columnist for the *Rapid City Journal*, a regional daily. Pat eventually joined me in Rapid City, where we married in 1992 and lived thereafter in a lovely woodsy glen in the Black Hills, ten miles south of town.

Eight years later, in 2000, I learned from Art Clark, an American editor I knew at Aramco (by then renamed Saudi Aramco), that a writer-editor job had opened in the company's Public Relations Department in Dhahran. Pat and I jumped at the chance for a new adventure—and I was excited to introduce my wife to my unique "hometown."

On December 19 of that year we were winging our way to Dhahran. It was just over nine months before 9/11, the infamous day fifteen Saudi nationals plus three other terrorists flew two commercial jetliners into the twin towers of New York's World Trade Center and a third into the Department of Defense Pentagon complex in Washington, D.C. The attacks killed nearly three thousand people and injured more than six thousand others, the deadliest domestic catastrophe in U.S. history.

GOING 'HOME' AGAIN, REDUX

Our friends and families had thought we were a little insane to join Aramco—even *before* 9/11. But fortunately, we were not dissuaded. The move back to the Kingdom proved to be a beautiful, beguiling, broadening experience. It was bathed in nostalgia and rendered far richer by the warm relationships we developed not only with Saudis—men, women and children alike—but new acquaintances from a wealth of cultures.

Like people everywhere, Saudis in general are unfailingly kind and loyal, and exceedingly generous. In fact, when our car broke down late one evening on the busy Dhahran-Khobar highway, a number of Saudis stopped to offer help, but none of the expatriates who sped past.

More than seventy nationalities were represented in Aramco at the cusp of the millennium. It was a veritable Tower of Babel in which, gratefully, everyone shared at least one language, English, the company's official *lingua franca*. Many non-native English speakers were perfectly at home, even eloquent and innovative, in English. But, to my ear, Saudis spoke it with the most subtle, understandable—even soothing—accent.

Today, Aramco (Saudi-owned since 1988, when renamed Saudi Aramco) generally mandates employee retirement at sixty. However, because of special manpower needs when I reached that age, the company granted me an additional year of service. Ultimately, I retired at sixty-one, in August 2011, and Pat and I returned to South Dakota. I don't know if we will ever see Saudi Arabia again, although Saudi Aramco sponsors periodic reunion events in the Kingdom for former employees (known as "annuitants") and "brats" (people who once grew up or lived in Aramco towns). We hope to attend one some day, "God willin' and the creek don't rise," as they say here in America's Midwestern prairie heartland (which, incidentally, used to be called The Great American Desert).

RETIREMENT IN AMERICA'S HEARTLAND

In the meantime, my wife and I are enjoying life on a pretty, wide creek in eastern South Dakota (our rescue cat named Razi, named after a radical tenth-century Muslim skeptic philosopher, shared the experience with us until he died suddenly in 2017).

We live amid many exotic and colorful artifacts and mementos of our time in Saudi Arabia and of global travels made possible by generous Aramco employment benefits as well as the Kingdom's close proximity—and, thus, budget travel access—to many of the wonders of the world and its greatest cities in Asia, Africa, Europe and parts less known.

Roughly forty percent of my life so far was spent in Saudi Arabia over three extremely different eras. To describe this as fortunate would be a huge understatement. The tripartite experience fundamentally shaped who I am, cementing my character for good and not too much, I hope, for ill.

THE INDIFFERENT AMERICAN

Regrettably, though, each time I returned to the U.S. after a stint in the Kingdom, I was reminded that many Americans lack curiosity about Saudi Arabia and, indeed, the wider world.

Many other "brats" tell me they've experienced that same blank reaction. It's disconcerting given the need for better understanding of the world's enormous and often conflicting diversity, which would promote more peaceful and tolerant collaboration with one another. My desire to encourage more American interest toward the rest of the world is partly what prompted me to write this book. How a tiny oil camp in the middle of Saudi Arabia's eastern coastal plain transformed the world is a neglected if transformative story worth telling. Oil, it turns out, is truly earth-shaking stuff, economically and culturally.

I also hope to preserve for posterity some sense of the unique phenomenon of Dhahran in the fifties and early sixties, this ephemeral, quasi-colonial American experiment. I wish to honor the country and people who helped inform my holistic worldview, and also to celebrate the experiences of other Aramcons who lived there, citizens of the world and not just one country.

Like politics, history is always essentially local.

Early Dhahran home. (Courtesy Saudi Aramco)

Home again, 1982.

My family leaving on vacation.

Bedouin tent in desert near Dhahran, 1950s. (Courtesy Saudi Aramco)

Expats shopping in Khobar, 1950s. (Courtesy Saudi Aramco)

Young Saudi men on Jeddah shore. (Doug Curran Photo)

Dhahran "main gate."
(Courtesy Saudi Aramco)

Me (middle) interviewed by Saudi reporters, 1982.

Dad arrives in Dhahran, 1953.

INTRODUCTION

FOR MOST AMERICANS, the first buoyant years after World War II were among the best of times.

Improbable as it may seem, life was particularly agreeable for those intrepid Yanks who found themselves living and working during the first two postwar decades in the scorched desert plains of eastern Saudi Arabia.

THE ADVENTURE BEGINS

By 1950 the horrors of World War II had largely receded, and America dominated the brave new, postwar world. The promising oilfields wild-catted just before the war by American geologists in the arid, menacing Arabian wastelands were by mid-century gushing oil and luring former grunts and sailors and flyboys like thirsty camels to a sudden waterhole.

The Americans arrived with their flat-top haircuts, still-lean warrior physiques and that can-do American confidence that anything—"anything in the world"—is do-able if you just refuse to quit. Soon, sporting desert tans streaked with dirt and sweat, and a potent, adventurous brio, they were hard at work creating something from nothing—as Americans from Jamestown to Los Alamos to the Panama Canal had always done.

What the American oilmen and their Saudi hosts ultimately achieved would prove to be nearly miraculous, unleashing the world-changing power of a virtual subterranean sea of "black gold." Coincidentally, it also inadvertently bequeathed to later generations the inevitable global warfare, social conflict and environmental degradation spawned by competition for and exploitation of a vital and precious yet innately toxic and planet-threatening fossil fuel.

MR. SNEDEKER GOES TO DHAHRAN

My father, Albert Coleman Snedeker, then twenty-nine, was assigned in 1949 to the new Arabian-American Oil Co. (Aramco) venture—a partnership of top American oil firms, including his employer, Standard Oil of California (SoCal).

In February 1953, Aramco transferred him from its New York office to field headquarters in Saudi Arabia. Because Aramco family housing was still under construction in Arabia, Dad had to temporarily leave the rest of us—my eldest sibling, Mike, nine; sister, Kathy, four; me, three; and Mom (the former Betty Brown)—behind in Walnut Creek, California. It was near where Dad grew up and his mother still lived. We left-behinds had moved from New York back to California when Dad departed for the desert.

We would join him about six months later in sunbaked Arabia, arriving on Aug. 7, 1953, at the fledgling Aramco-built airfield near Dhahran, roughly four miles inland from Saudi Arabia's eastern Persian Gulf coast.

When Dad arrived in Dhahran (pronounced *dah-RAHN*) in 1953, the embryonic community still resembled a glorified roustabout oil camp, which was why its residents referred to it as "the camp." Like many young American men migrating to the oil fields and boomtowns that were rapidly proliferating in Arabia, my father presented a striking figure: six-foot-two, 185 pounds, ripped with the still-defined muscle mass of a college athlete.

I remember the controlled, purposeful way he walked, with just a hint of an athlete's coiled swagger, revealing a natural confidence that briskly implied, "No problem, I've got this."

Basic-but-comfortable Dhahran camp, a place unique in American history, would become our home for the next nine years. The move culminated a series of eventful progressions for my father and the beginning of a new, transformative life for his family.

THE ROAD TO SAUDI

On May 11, 1941, just seven months before Japan's devastating military attack on Pearl Harbor, Dad had been awarded a bachelor's degree in business administration at St. Mary's College, a small Catholic liberal arts school in northern California. The twenty-one-year-old graduate immediately enlisted in the U.S. Navy's officer candidate school, began pilot training and soon ended up in the South Pacific theater.

During the war, Dad flew PBY Catalinas, long-range reconnaissance "flying boats" designed to take off and land in water, hopping from one remote atoll base to another, looking for Japanese warships. The planes ("PB" stood for "patrol bomber") were also used for torpedo bombing, convoy escort and other tasks. After the war, Dad joined the Navy Reserves and was hired by SoCal in California. He briefly had considered joining one of the new commercial airlines as a pilot but feared it would seem, compared to exciting war-time flying, "like driving a bus."

POSTWAR BOOM

In the early days of the postwar American renaissance, many Americans flocked to Arabia seeking work and money.

These were mostly bachelors, along with a few married men such as my father whose families were temporarily marooned in the States.

The adventurous Yanks, now Aramco employees, started building residential camps and industrial facilities for themselves and equipment for petroleum extraction and refining on eastern Arabia's sprawling low sandstone *jebels* and desert *sabkha* (salt flats).

Construction crews were feverishly building houses for families anxiously waiting to come—and for some of the single men who hoped to start a family soon. Dhahran in those days looked much like historical videos of the camp-like Manhattan Project community in Los Alamos, New Mexico, where American scientists developed and built atomic bombs during the war. All plywood, screen doors, and dust.

Early Dhahran exuded the spare ambience of a military encampment, but the Aramco oilmen in the Saudi desert sensed they might be there a lot longer than the nuclear scientists stayed in New Mexico's high-desert wastelands during the war years.

Colonial 'lite'

Aramco represented a somewhat uncommon phenomenon in U.S. history—a kind of American colonial presence, something akin to the British Raj in India in the nineteenth and twentieth centuries. In past eras, America had controlled a number of colonial enclaves and occupation zones, generally temporary and evolving from warfare (and sometimes commercial interests). These included parts of the Philippines, Puerto Rico, Cuba, and Nicaragua, Japan, and in Europe after World War II (e.g., West Berlin), as well as islands in the South Pacific.

Aramco's mid-century presence in Arabia, however, approximated what might be described as Colonialism Lite, an arguably kinder, gentler, less imperial and authoritarian construct than those elsewhere. At least, Aramcons would like to have thought so.

However, just as the Raj exploited Indian agricultural products and native labor for British profit, Aramco's partners exploited the Saudi Kingdom's abundant oil and native manpower for American profit. It was the holy grail of capitalism: colossal risk chasing unfathomable wealth.

The 'hunch'

The search for Arabian oil began in 1934 with a hunch by Max Steineke, a rough-hewn American SoCal geologist. His experience and gut feeling—coalescing in a famous hunch—convinced him that oceans of oil lay beneath the desolate sands of Arabia's eastern deserts.

Commercially viable quantities of oil had been discovered in 1933 by a SoCal subsidiary, California-Arabian Standard Oil Co. (Casoc), on the island of Bahrain just fifteen miles offshore Arabia. To Steineke's experienced eye, the terrain in Saudi Arabia looked tantalizingly similar to that on Bahrain. Investors decided to "go for it," but the going was tough.

In 1938—at the proverbial "eleventh hour," as investors grew nervous after a string of dry holes—well No. 7 at Dhahran started flowing a commercially encouraging 1,500 barrels per day. This heartened the Aramco partners to keep production flowing on No. 7 while drilling new wildcat wells elsewhere in the area.

The high-stakes gamble ultimately paid off handsomely for then American-owned Aramco, and for future American prosperity and influence in the world, as well as for Saudi Arabia and its people. Who got the better deal is for history to decide.

World beating

Today Saudi Aramco is the world's most valuable company, based solely on its accessible oil reserves. *The Economist,* the respected British magazine, has estimated the company's value at about $2.25 *trillion.* In 2016, *The Wall Street Journal* reckoned that Aramco's value could be as high as $10 trillion, roughly twenty times greater than Exxon's. At the time, this made the estimated value of mighty Apple Inc., the creator of iPhone, look paltry at $600 billion.

The Kingdom today leads the world in oil exports and readily accessible reserves of proven conventional crude oil and condensate (oil derived from gas production). A single Aramco-discovered oil field, Ghawar in Saudi Arabia's Eastern Province, has consistently been able to produce five million barrels of oil a day since the 1950s, roughly half of the company's total normal output. At nineteen miles wide and 174 miles long, gargantuan Ghawar is by far the largest oil field on the planet.

Despite its necessity at the onset, the American presence in the company and the Kingdom has gradually faded over the years. Americans now represent a tiny though essential minority of the oil company's 65,282 employees, eighty-five percent of whom are Saudi nationals (based on most recent corporate figures). The ten thousand expatriate employees represent scores of different nationalities. The mammoth enterprise, by far the world's largest energy company, has been wholly Saudi-owned since 1988. At that time the company completed a buyout of American partners and rebranded itself as Saudi Aramco.

The Kingdom today also is among the world's top ten in natural gas reserves and production. However, its gas output generally feeds internal demand rather than exports, much of it for petrochemical production and electric power.

HINDSIGHT

In retrospect, Saudis may feel that the Aramco presence in their Kingdom over the years was benignly paternal or exploitive, or culturally damaging, or shades of all.

But for Americans living there, especially in the fifties and early sixties, the expatriate boomtown charm of the Aramco lifestyle felt like a kind of understated suburban utopia. Luxury camping with servants. Unlike Aramco's other relatively drab, parched camps nearby, Dhahran was the administrative hub. As such the admin camp had evolved into a lush oasis, almost startling against the endless sun-bleached sand and *sabkha*.

Desert flowers sometimes bloomed beyond the community's demarcating fence-line after an infrequent rain. Like Arizona badlands after a gully washer.

A NEW NATION

The Saudi nation was founded in 1932 when charismatic Ibn Saud finally consolidated his control over the far-flung cities, towns and tribal groups of his sprawling, lightly populated desert realm. The Red Sea bookended the new country on its western coast and the Persian Gulf to the east.

The desert nation has scant rainfall and many scorched zones that precipitation routinely ignores for decades; then as now the country lacks permanent lakes or rivers.

Undeterred by the country's barren, grinding poverty, Ibn Saud exhibited keen prescience and shrewd optimism. He saw in a partnership with the Americans the possibility of enormous political and economic potential for himself, his country and his people. And history proved him right.

COMING TO ARABIA

I am told I was a rambunctious toddler in 1953 when our family flew into the modest airport Aramco was developing near Dhahran.

As we stepped off the plane, late summer assaulted us like dragon's breath, the flaming humidity literally hair-curling. Usual for that time of year, the temperature would have been 113-115° F with 75%-90% humidity. I distinctly remember walking out of the cool interior of the airplane and being blast-furnaced by scorching desert air plus the 160° or more radiating off the tarmac. August is always a sweltering swamp in Dhahran.

But, for me, the absolute highlight of that debut journey was the thrill of flying in one of Aramco's three McDonnell-Douglas DC-6 four-prop planes that had been cozily refitted as company airliners. I have no idea which of the glorious trio we flew in—the aptly named Flying Camel, Flying Gazelle or Flying Oryx—but the transcendent experience far exceeded just "loud." Especially the deafening takeoffs and landings, and the weird but exhilarating new sense I experienced of actually leaving Earth.

On that first arrival, my folks said later, they expected us to stay in Dhahran several years. The classical Arabic tale *Arabian Nights* famously spanned 1,001 nights; we ended up staying more than 3,001, about nine years.

Because I was so young when we came to Arabia, I have only a few initial memories, and those are probably a little suspect, cross-contaminated by family stories, photographs, home movies and the erosions of passing time. But I clearly remember brand-new Dhahran neighborhoods in progress: poured concrete walkways transcribing scores of empty, rectangular sand lots where houses would soon be built. It appeared as if city-block-wide grids of concrete had simply been dropped from a helicopter on virgin desert sand.

Indeed, sand and its flighty cousin, dust, contaminated everything in Dhahran. Grit stealthily seeped into homes, covering surfaces anew with finely powdered dirt only seconds after it had been dusted away. Airborne crunchies stuck fast to the undersides of our eyelids, within nostrils, between teeth. Dust filled auto air filters and clogged engines, invaded lungs and dulled colors. Mixed with humidity, sand and dust became oily, noxious, ineradicable grime. Early on, the granular, adhesive stuff relentlessly hounded everything and everyone in Arabia, stalking, mocking us. The arch-enemy of clean.

DHAHRAN EMERGES FROM THE SAND

Soon buildings appeared in the empty lots, and folks learned ways to partially keep the sand at bay, if not the flies.

The flies, however, posed only a short-lived inconvenience, as little Aramco maintenance vehicles soon smoked our neighborhoods with dense, choking clouds of insecticide. The flies never had a chance. We had no idea then that the stuff might be dangerous to *us*. After all,

Rachel Carson's groundbreaking *Silent Spring*, which raised the specter of chemical catastrophe from pesticides, wouldn't be published for nearly a decade hence.

Before long, Dhahran felt like home, albeit an exotic one. For kids, the experience somewhat resembled the movie *The Truman Show*, whose *faux* town had been created for a television series in which the townspeople and viewers knew of the deceit, but the clueless star, Truman, did not. Yet, as Aramcons, residents of Dhahran, we were a happy lot, enjoying with little analysis our semi-utopian existence in the Arabian desert in the graceful, hopeful era of Elvis, *The Catcher in the Rye* and Eisenhower.

What a camp out!

SAUDI ARABIA TODAY

Years later, toward the end of the twentieth century and into the twenty-first, the already tense, murderous situation in the Middle East steadily deteriorated.

The main driver of the instability was intensifying acts of war and terror primarily by Muslim radicals in Arab nations surrounding Israel (also an instigator of violence and terror), largely fueled by Palestinians' unending existential struggle with Israel over its continuing occupation of their traditional territories and injustices toward them. The Islamic world largely, and accurately, sees America as Israel's powerful enabler.

But the mistrust can flow both ways. Western opinion of Saudi Arabia, for example, cratered following the Khobar Towers atrocity in 1996, particularly after the Sept. 11, 2001, attacks on America led predominantly by Saudi *jihadists*. I clearly remember learning of both incidents with enormous incredulity, having spent many years in the Kingdom and routinely being befriended by unfailingly warm, kind, gentle Saudis. Where, in God's name, had such evil been hiding during the nearly two decades I had already lived there, I wondered?

I prefer to always think of Saudi Arabia—as my personal experiences consistently reaffirmed—as a welcoming place teeming with friendly, devout inhabitants. It was so safe you could walk down the darkest street in the largest city in the dead of night with the *riyal* equivalent of a thousand dollars in your pocket and never worry about being mugged. Indeed, expats generally carried a chunk of cash for unforeseen emergencies, which almost never occurred.

It was a place where a young woman in a traditional market area would instantly have one hundred indignant champions at her disposal if any man or boy even mildly annoyed her. Where families were large, intertwined and devoted. Where public violence seemed vanishingly rare. Certainly, life is complicated, and all people can be erratic and hateful, even brutal, when certain primal impulses are triggered, but during my times in Saudi Arabia I never saw anything that remotely seemed to foreshadow a 9/11-style political atrocity.

But this is not a book about dreadful politics. It is, instead, a memoir of fond remembrance.

Saudi works on Aramco oil well. (Courtesy Saudi Aramco)

Saudi trainees exit Aramco school,
1950s. (Courtesy Saudi Aramco)

First president Tom Barger in field. (Courtesy Saudi Aramco)

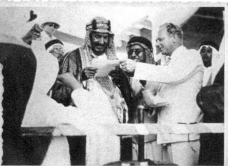

Ibn Saud, the new nation's first king, honors
first oil shipment, 1939. (Courtesy Saudi Aramco)

Incomparable Aramco guide Khamis
ibn Rimthan. (Courtesy Saudi Aramco)

Wide Dhahran streets, tidy bungalows. (Courtesy Saudi Aramco)

Legendary Aramco geologist Max Steineke (left). (Courtesy Saudi Aramco)

Me and giant Aramco desert truck.

Dhahran's post office. (Courtesy Saudi Aramco)

CHAPTER 1

THE CAMP

IN THE TRANQUIL, unhurried mid-century period, Aramcons informally called Dhahran "the camp" when we were encamped there. But when away from the Kingdom, something invisible changed, and we temporarily—inexplicably, as far as I could tell—renamed it "the field."

Yet it was always the exact same place.

After a vacation in the U.S., for example, my folks would tell their American friends and extended families, "We'll be returning to *the field* next week." As in "oil field," I guessed.

But, once back in Dhahran, it was for some peculiar reason suddenly "the camp" again.

"Whatcha say we head back to *camp*?" Dad would ask Mom after a day with the kids dodging jellyfish and building sand castles at Half Moon Bay beach on the Gulf.

But no matter what we called it, Dhahran was magical.

'Main Street, Arabia'

A central area of town housed Aramco's administrative offices along with the usual assortment of civic amenities found in small American stateside communities.

Everything was company-subsidized and cheap, and exuded a military-base vibe, owing to the American postwar ex-servicemen who originally put the place together.

"Main Street" amenities included the:

- **Mail Center:** the post office.

- **Barber shop:** with Indian and Arab barbers—and shaves!

- **Commissary:** the local grocery store (my dad's job was to make sure it was fully stocked by ordering and tracking delivery of foodstuffs from around the world).

- **King's Road Stadium:** the verdant, well-manicured main baseball field where I played Little League and Dad participated in overhand-pitching adult softball leagues.

- **Theater:** where I learned to love movies, like my father, who took us there several times each week when the main feature changed, especially before TV arrived in Dhahran in 1958. Community Theater productions were also staged there along with some school and community presentations, plus various Catholic and Protestant church services on Friday (the end of the Islamic week, which Aramco observed).

- **Bowling alley:** twelve lanes, lots of leagues, and "pin boys" to reset knocked-over pins. Where I spent many happy hours bowling by myself. Cost about thirty cents (one Saudi *riyal*) per game, plus fifteen *girsh*, a few cents, for shoes.

- **Fiesta Room:** The best milk shakes, burgers and French fries on the planet, without question. We blew our shake-dipped straw wrappers onto the ceiling, where they hung until the cooks retrieved them.

- **Library:** You could literally hear a pin drop in that place. It felt like a church.

- **Swimming pool:** a large, beautiful pool with Indian lifeguards, covered at one end against the raging sun. An adjacent snack bar sold little Dixie Cups of frozen vanilla ice cream that you chipped at with a tiny paddle-shaped wooden spoon.

- **Open-air community dance floor:** Located next to the pool, its polished concrete surface drew Aramco couples to evening dances under the stars, especially in the early years. Tuxedos and party dresses were once the norm; I have pictures of my folks, dressed to the nines, at a dance there.

- **Rolling Hills Golf Course:** Though low, hills actually exist within Dhahran. Although grass was planted at the golf course after the turn of the millennia, for most of the town's history the course made-do with "natural" fairways (meaning desert) and oil-blackened greens. Players carried a piece of fake turf to hit from and not scuff their clubs on the hard desert *sabkah*. Saudis initially served as caddies, sometimes using long-legged white donkeys from nearby Hofuf to carry players' golf bags. White golf balls would have been perpetually lost in the bleached-out landscape, so red balls graced Rolling Hills.

Add to all that comfortable, well-appointed homes, a U.S.-accredited school system, a strong sense of community, and a general feeling of security and safety in company camps and facilities, and you had all the makings of an enviable life in mid-century Aramco "camps."

Even beyond that warm community cocoon, things were interesting and exotic.

BEYOND

To picture the arid landscape just *beyond* Dhahran's circumscribing fence in those days, think of eastern California's Mojave Desert, an endlessly beige and hard-packed landscape virtually devoid of foliage except for the occasional bunch of what we American expats in Saudi Arabia called "camel grass." Just a dusty poof of washed-out green here and there in the endless, flat, dun-colored monotony.

Yet in the Kingdom's Eastern Province coastal plain, enchanting beauty married stern desolation where Aramco's Dhahran headquarters community stood out like a bright green surprise. A vibrant sign of life in the bland infinity.

Fewer than five miles east of camp, the salty, shallow, seemingly inviting waters of the Persian Gulf twinkled on the horizon. But despite mild air temperatures in winter, the waterway itself was generally too chilly to swim in that time of year and far too Jacuzzi-hot much of the blazing summer for a pleasurable dip. The experience was even more odious when coupled with dripping humidity and sand in your underpants. What a waste, I always thought.

And the Gulf provided a poor vista as well; a constant haze hung over the waterway for much of summer, dulling the water's natural sapphire hue and obscuring the brilliant sky. But in more temperate months the Gulf waters brightened, the sky turned baby blue, and clouds sailed by gloriously white and huge.

Still, the Gulf rarely if ever seemed to achieve a goldilocks temperature for swimming. However, Dad and Mom sometimes took us to the beach to frolic in the too-warm water, making us wear T-shirts against the burning sun. Salt tablets were distributed.

KHOBAR

In the old days, the only other pockets of "civilization" in the area besides Dhahran were the indigenous Saudi towns of Dammam and al-Khobar, sixty and fifteen minutes away, respectively, and the Aramco camps of Ras Tanura (where the refinery was located) and Abqaiq (near the gigantic Ghawar oil field), each about an hour.

As a young boy, I often accompanied my family on the short drive east from Dhahran to pungent al-Khobar (*al-KO-bar*) on the Gulf shore. It's dirt "main street" was lined with ramshackle, half-finished concrete-block buildings on either side. There may have been other streets and structures, but we usually just hung out on the unnamed main drag, where most of the little sand-strewn shops were located and barefoot, crusty-heeled money-changers squatted on low stools. The town had a complex, invigorating aroma of sea air, undeodorized sweat, exotic incense and strange spices set out in the open air, which the heat and engulfing stillness rendered ever muskier, especially in summer. I found the aroma mysterious and a bit intoxicating.

The only marginally distinctive feature on the dusty road to Khobar and back was a single concrete-block gas station about halfway, identical in color and texture to the desert. If you blinked, you missed it; it blended so well with its surroundings, you could barely make it out even if you planned to stop there for gas.

Sometimes a camel or two glanced at us listlessly from the distance as we drove by. Occasionally a big, fat *daub*, a lizard like the Arizona Gila monster but chubbier and the color of sand, might stare at us motionless from the roadside, blinking nervously.

Community dances were big entertainment in early Dhahran. (Courtesy Saudi Aramco)

Learning to mount a camel. (Courtesy Saudi Aramco)

Aramco truck overwhelms tiny Messerschmitt
in Dhahran. (Courtesy Saudi Aramco)

Dhahran commissary in camp's
early days. (Courtesy Saudi Aramco)

Kathy and I seesawing at playground.

Dhahran polo match on
donkeys. (Courtesy Saudi Aramco)

Dhahran street scene. (Courtesy Saudi Aramco)

Washing off the gulf salt in Ras Tanura.

Snedeker Christmas photo, mid-1950s.

OUR FAMILY

A S FAR AS I could tell, my family was so normal it was boring. *Leave It To Beaver*-like.

It didn't occur to me when we all reunited in Arabia in 1953—Dad and Mom, Mike, Kathy and me, ages thirty-three, thirty-one, nine, four and three—that we were anything *but*. Everyone in our extended family in the U.S. thought we were nuts to go live in an alien desert wilderness far beyond civilization, beset by hardship and want.

But it wasn't like that at all.

At first, like everyone else in Dhahran, we had a servant from India, a "houseboy." That was just a tease, though. Several years after our arrival, my folks arbitrarily decided "for your own good" (meaning us kids' "good") to banish these incredibly useful people from our house. Significantly, our house *alone* dispensed with houseboys; all the neighbors, rationally, kept theirs. (More on this in Chapter 17.)

After the Great Houseboy Banishment, we Snedeker kids were required to wash and dry dishes, mow the lawn and make our beds; we were also allowed to run and scream *only* outdoors (houseboys didn't care where we did that); and there were many other new rules, which we always—well, generally—followed.

Dad and Mom provided a house to live in, rules to live by, prepared meals, negotiated family decisions and organized vacations. Our job was to obey.

So, even though we found ourselves at the end of earth, watching camels amble about in the distance, it was totally fine. Our town was safe, our house solid, the beds not-too-soft, and we had plenty to eat. Even ice cream. For kids, it was perfect.

Leave It To Beaver, like I said.

Dressed up in Hong Kong.

Us kids at Grandma Dolly's Lafayette house.

Family photo, minus Dad.

Visiting Mom's dad, Grandpa Brown, in Oregon.

Front yard, 4491-B.

Budding cat person.

Playing with friends in our yard.

Returning to the U.S. with Grandma Dolly.

Dad in Dhahran, like *Mad Men's* rakish "Don Draper."

C H A P T E R 3

DAD

A HANDSOME, FRIENDLY GUY the ladies seemed to like a lot, Dad was also a good Catholic who believed strongly in "doing the right thing," as he frequently reiterated. Anyone could see that he only had eyes for Mom.

He hardly ever left home alone except to work; one of us always shadowed him otherwise. "Big Al," as some called him, was a steadfast family guy. I just couldn't see how he could possibly have found the time for that *other* stuff, at least after I became aware that there *was* other stuff.

LIKE CLOCKWORK

Dad lived like clockwork, a habit he picked up from the Navy, I suspect. He rose at the same time every morning, 5:45 on the dot (his eyes automatically sprang open *without* an alarm), ate a leisurely breakfast with Mom from 6:30-7:30 (we kids had to stay in our bedrooms so they could have "privacy," whatever *that* meant). Then began his ultra-predictable workday, arriving at the office at 8 and leaving at 5, then arriving home in time to get ready for dinner at 6 sharp. A community siren blared at noon and 5, sounding like a police car in the 1955-1959 TV drama *Highway Patrol* starring Broderick Crawford.

Before dinner, Mom invariably joined Dad for a "highball" and potato chips. The cocktails were concocted with Dad's potent home-made moonshine (locally known as *sidiqi*, "my friend" in Arabic and pro-nounced *sih-DEE-kee*). Alcohol was (and still is) banned in the Kingdom because it's prohibited by Islam, but the government apparently looked the other way if Aramcons made their own—as nearly everyone did—and marshalled its sometimes problematic effects discreetly within com-pany compounds.

Dad always fell asleep watching the TV news at 9:50 or so. Then he would complain, "Hey, I was watching that!" when my Mom turned the TV off at 10 to wake him. He would shuffle into bed around 10:10.

Same thing next day, and the next, until the weekend, when he only worked a half-day on Thursdays (Aramco weekends were Thursday-Friday, the Saudi weekend).

THE COLOR-CODED WARDROBE

This straight-laced uniformity affected Dad's wardrobe as well.

He segregated his sock drawer by color and arranged pairs according to hue color and intensity, lights gradated to darks. Same with shirts and pants and suits. His closet and drawers looked master-planned to me. His leather wing-tip and penny-loafer shoes were always polished to a nice sheen, using one of those steel shoe-shine contraptions that looked like a giant Erector Set praying mantis. I didn't inherit Dad's hyper-organized, tidy compulsions. Fortunately. My wardrobe organizing prin-ciple is, "If I ever, even by mistake, organize anything by color, please shoot me."

As a committed father and former star athlete, Dad encouraged Mike and me to play sports but, surprisingly, never pushed us, not that he had to; we lived for sports. He taught us how to hit and catch base-balls, shoot and dribble basketballs, and he traveled to all our games when we joined organized teams. As president of the Arabian American Little League a couple of years, he shot miles of eight-millimeter film of our games, and everyone anticipated his year-end film montage, the high-light of the annual awards banquets (whoever was shown in the video felt famous). He drove us to Little League games in the other camps, played in the annual father-son game and gently critiqued our on-field performances during the season. The fundamental importance in my life of his unfailing support didn't dawn on me until much later, though.

At the annual Arabian Little League Father-Son Game, the dads had to run the bases on crutches. It was a visual punch line; the conceit was that the dads were so old they could only run the bases with the aid of crutches. Even funnier, they tried to run normally while carrying the crutches like suitcases.

'RISE AND SHINE'

My father personified sunny optimism. In fact, even his juvenile nick-name was "Sonny." Close enough.

Dad unfailingly awoke upbeat every morning of my childhood; on school days he breezed into the bedroom I shared with Mike, flipped on the light, and two steps later simultaneously yanked the covers off both our peacefully slumbering forms. "Rise and shine, it's breakfast time!" he sang in his rich, baritone voice.

Although not chatty, my father was always present, the guy who generally showed you how to be a guy, not by talk but deed. And prac-tical simplicity characterized all his guidance: Control yourself. Be cour-teous. Be honest but don't gossip. Don't hit girls. Don't act like a moron. Don't be a know-it-all, either. Don't brag. Don't ever start a fight (but be damn sure you end one someone else starts). Deliver a firm handshake.

Don't hug boys. Never—*ever*—bring shame or disrepute on the family. Be nice to your sister. Kiss your mother good night. Stuff like that.

Strangely, years later in my fourties when reuniting with my family in Arizona after a long absence in Arabia, my dad, most unexpectedly, hugged me at the airport, like we'd been doing it our whole lives. Weird. Totally against the rules. Which *he* made, by the way. But, still, it was surprisingly poignant.

BIRTHDAY SUITS

Without saying a word, Dad also taught all of us kids to consider the unclothed human body as a completely normal, natural thing, and that being caught in your "birthday suit" was no big deal; no deal at all, in fact.

When we were little, we used to sit around the bathroom as Dad—"a la September morn," as he described his "birthday suit"—shaved after his shower, dispensing occasional wisdom and wisecracks. His casual nudity seemed the most natural thing in the world. Yet Mom—Pluto to Dad's Uranus regarding personal modesty—could be counted on to execute a swan dive behind the bed if we happened to walk in on her in *her* birthday suit.

So, I remain a little conflicted by the mixed messages, simultaneously thinking that mowing your unfenced front yard in the nude should be an acceptable practice while at the same time wondering why anyone would ever do such a thing.

SELF-UNPLEASURING

One odd, perplexing occurrence underscored this modesty divide between Dad and Mom.

I was maybe six, sitting in the bathtub alone one night, absent-mindedly checking out my anatomy, as little boys do, poking and pulling at this and that, oblivious that larger issues might be involved.

My Mom happened to come in, saw this purportedly terrifying behavior and, apparently ... insisted Dad make me stop. He soon appeared next to the tub, hulking over me like Goliath, but looking *really* uncomfortable. He said I probably shouldn't be poking and pulling at this and that. And then he left. Made no sense at all to me.

So, thereafter, I just tried to ignore myself.

MAN IN A HURRY

In addition to very dutiful husbanding, Dad was also whip-smart and fearless, finishing high school at sixteen, graduating college at twenty and piloting U.S. Navy patrol bombers at twenty-one in World War II.

After the war, he worked for Standard Oil of California, SoCal for short (Dad's mother, my Grandma Dolly, purportedly befriended the company's president, and the topic of marriage reportedly came up at some point, but Grandma demurred). Having already suffered through the recent long, painful death of her first husband—"Grandpa Father," to me—my grandmother loathed the prospect of nursing another spouse into the grave. Or so the story goes.

Dad was later promoted and transferred to SoCal's New York office, soon finding himself in the desert of Saudi Arabia in 1953, at thirty-three.

His job with Aramco, he once explained to me, involved managing the timely shipping, receiving and stocking of supplies that sustained the Dhahran community. Like toilet paper, baby oil and, most importantly, Pep Flakes (more on this later).

MORALITY TALE

As the main purchaser of Dhahran residential commodities, Dad attracted the attention of people who sometimes didn't subscribe to his particular code of chivalrous, ethical behavior and thought nothing of bribing or *otherwise* enticing people if it meant landing a big Aramco supply contract.

He told me about a well-known Saudi entrepreneur who did business with Aramco and tried to entice Dad into buying his merchandise by inviting him to a free, lavish weekend of partying on the island of Bahrain, some fifteen miles offshore. Dad didn't ever party without Mom, and—as he told me—he strongly suspected "party girls" would attend the Bahrain shindig. I didn't see the problem—parties certainly must need "party girls," I assumed at that young age. But I could tell by the way Dad told the story, that *he* certainly saw them as not only not needed, but to be very wary of. Either way, he stayed home.

This story exemplified an invaluable and mathematically precise life lesson: People offering free stuff = risk. And a related axiom: The more tempting the free stuff = the bigger the risk.

Handy as well as bright, Dad could make or repair just about anything. Unfortunately, we were banned from "helping" in his home projects because he, rationally, feared disruption if not destruction of his handiwork at our hands. Necessarily then, I grew up decidedly *not* handy, certainly ill-equipped to build, as my dad did, a lovingly crafted scale-model replica of the life-size house being built in the U.S. for our return in 1962.

CHARACTER

Dad also bequeathed to me a glimpse of the character of his own father, who fate decided I would never meet. The day my mother confirmed my budding presence in her womb, she and my dad learned that Grandpa Father, a longtime chain smoker, had died. Lung cancer.

To cope with unbearable pain during his extended battle with the insidious disease, I'm told Grandpa became a Christian Science adherent, calling a "reader" for support when icy fingers of agony routinely gripped his body.

My dad once told of accompanying his father one night to pick up his paycheck at the *San Francisco Chronicle*, where he worked as an editor in the depths of the Great Depression. The city at the time teemed with desperate, unemployed men, and it was a minor miracle that grandfather was employed at all. But, still, it paid a pittance and required him to live the whole workweek in the city, returning home only on weekends to his home and family in the far-away little inland hamlet of Lafayette.

After retrieving his paycheck at the *Chronicle* that night, Grandpa and my dad walked down an alley toward their car, when a stranger emerged from the shadow of a doorway, asking, "Hey, bud, got a light?" Dad recalled his father courteously replied "No, sorry" to the stranger and then, looking straight ahead, whispered to my dad, "Keep walking, son." My dad said he felt the hair on the back of his neck stand up, and goosebumps crawl across his shoulders and down his arms. A brand-new idea had suddenly occurred to him at that moment: unapparent dangers exist in the world.

Dad also told a charming story about Grampa Father's tendency toward moral gallantry that reflected in Dad's own nature. A rabid anti-Communist, his father nonetheless once agreed to take my dad and some of his friends to a movie at Lafayette theater starring Edward G. Robinson, a "commie pinko"—a Communist, a "Red" (per the color of the movement's flag)—in Grampa's estimation. The inveterate Red-baiter sat patiently in the theater lobby the entire movie, and then without any noticeable rancor, drove the kids home afterward without comment.

During the Depression years, Grandpa lived in a dodgy flophouse, my dad said, and ate poorly when he worked in the city, to ensure he had money left over each week to send to his wife and family. As a result, the rest of the family survived more robustly than he did during that lean era, but, according to Dad, his father's health became permanently compromised before the economy rebounded.

You could see it in his face's deepening lines, he told us.

THE FAMILY MAN

I'm supremely lucky; I had a dad who was always present. A solid guy who cared about his family—clearly above all else. Who would do anything to protect and care for us. A guy who by living an honorable, useful life instilled a sense of honor and purpose in his kids.

The greatest practical inheritance, though, may have been the adventurous streak that fatefully led him to a trackless desert, thousands of miles from home and a key role supporting the development of a historic American endeavor that would have far-reaching global consequences.

My father's innate audacity deeply informed my childhood and later made me willing, even eager, to take similar risks as an adult, which eventually led back to where it all started: Dhahran. Full circle.

Curiously, the first time I returned to the Kingdom as an adult, in 1982—living in al-Khobar, though, not Dhahran—I had just turned thirty-two, about a year younger than Dad was when he first arrived in Arabia in 1953. I love that coincidence.

A GOOD DAY TO DIE

My Dad died unexpectedly (he seemed to still be going strong) and, from all accounts, instantaneously, in 1998 at seventy-eight. It was probably a massive coronary, or a stroke, the doctors vaguely and unhelpfully speculated, noting he had survived a heart attack nearly twenty years earlier, at fifty-nine.

As Dad had wished, he just suddenly ceased to be, no long, grueling goodbye that traumatized everyone he loved for weeks or months or years. No final war of attrition against uncaring nature. He also hoped to still be usefully engaged when it happened; at the exact moment of his passing, he was calling an insurance company to dispute a medical bill.

Frugal to the end, Dad pre-opted for a basic gurney at a brief, private wake before cremation, instead of a fancy brass-appointed, exotic-wood coffin and an elaborate public funeral. As I took my turn to say goodbye,

I resented the gurney's stark inelegance, which so spectacularly failed to fairly characterize the richness and even nobility of my father's life.

Although the unfussy moment did honor his essential modesty, it also ignored a curious, discordant mystery: he was inexplicably known on occasion to wear scarlet jump suits, pink sport jackets and colorfully striped, knee-high crew socks (sometimes even matching the color of Mom's outfits).

His head rested face-up on a foam block as he reclined in serene repose on the mortuary gurney, and gravity pulled his long, limp, silver hair straight back, severely, as though he was in a wind tunnel. Gravity also tugged backward on his face, necessarily giving him what appeared to be a wide, sunny smile.

For some reason, that scene reminded me of when we used to take family road trips in America in my youth. Dad, always impatient to get where we were going, often drove all night. When he thought everyone was asleep—except me, unbeknownst to him (I was afraid I might miss something)—this big, athletic, macho man often turned some radio music on low and sang along in a soft, soulful falsetto, smiling with contentment.

As he "smiled" on that gurney those many years later, I grinned and touched his hand one last time.

Arriving at his Dhahran office. (Courtesy Saudi Aramco)

Sporting WWII goatee,
bomber jacket.

Riding in a Hong
Kong rickshaw.

With brother Frank in Hawaii.

Dad's parents, Al and Marie ("Dolly"), 1940s.

Dad, Uncle Jimmy, Grandpa
Brown in WWII.

With siblings in childhood.

With his boys at 4491-B.

With Kathy in tow at Tri-District Fair.

Flirting with Mom during the war.

Dad's good friend Abdul Fatah Kabli.
(Courtesy Saudi Aramco)

Mom and brother Jim.

CHAPTER 4

MOM

As a young woman, she was a beauty. Long, wavy auburn hair in those great '40s styles; softly chiseled, aristocratic features; a look of genuine innocence. I've seen the pictures. Even I can see what turned my dad's head when he met her in high school.

As a mom, though, the raggedness of her wounded innocence is what stood out for me, an edgy, damaged, passive-aggressive quality that survived endless childhood assaults that probably should have destroyed her. She exuded wariness and guilelessness simultaneously, which I attributed to the sins of her self-absorbed parents who both repeatedly betrayed her trust and, from all evidence, failed to teach her even necessary rudiments of real life.

THE FRENCH KISS

Mom once told me a curious story, which she was wont to do, about some actual French guy she briefly dated as a teenager.

"He tried to French kiss me, and I didn't even know what that *was* at the time," she said, "so I jumped out of his Studebaker immediately and told him in no uncertain terms, 'Never try that again, ever, buster.'" I'm pretty sure her own racy mom knew *exactly* what it was but had somehow failed to usefully transfer the information to her daughter. The most interesting part of the story to me was that Mom remembered the car's brand.

Thus massively ill-informed, Mom tried to conform our family to her idealized version of family that a toxic brew of childhood pain and neglect, and an unrequited longing for familial contentment, had apparently synthesized in her mind. At least that's my interpretation. We never approached the perfection she craved, of course, but she nonetheless succeeded against all odds in creating a whole and reliably upright family, one with parents who diligently tried to instill decency and necessary knowledge, and a solid moral core. Kudos to her for that.

She was the designated presenter of "the talk" about the birds and bees to my sister and me one uncomfortable night when I was eight or nine, as I recall (as Dad was literally hidden behind a newspaper he was "reading"). She didn't mince words, I must report, liberally using previously banished terms like "penis" and "vagina" as necessary for full disclosure, and also describing new, eye-opening ways adults apparently employed those organs.

In retrospect, I think she was actually trying in some way to reimburse the world for the sins of omission of her parents, an entirely noble endeavor, if achingly sad and futile. But I think we kids sometimes benefitted from it greatly.

THE 'PERFECT' FAMILY

I always felt pressure in the Snedeker household to be better than we actually were. Which might actually have been a good thing. Maybe I turned out better and happier than I might've otherwise. Who knows? But I always had a hard time catering to Mom's idealized version of us.

Even though Mom provided our moral compass (even Dad said so), he seemed to me at least as good a person as her.

Even affection seemed more learned for her than natural. When we were young, Mom hugged and kissed us routinely—it was required that we reciprocate at bedtime, for example—but it had a subtly detached, compliant quality, although we never doubted we were loved. Nonetheless, her innate diffidence probably resulted in our developing a natural reserve toward her as well.

It's not that Mom lacked passion for her kids' welfare—she didn't. It just seemed as though children were somewhat alien beings to her— her parents' examples only illustrated what should be rigorously avoided, not embraced, in child-rearing. So she, as many new mothers in her generation, turned unquestioningly to Dr. Spock. And to untested intuition. Mom's strategy seemed to be that if she raised her kids to treat her with the affectionate respect she imagined mothers should be treated, all would be well in her world.

The problem is that affectionate respect is a sentiment nurtured, not a skill taught. I believe that, bereft of any useful wisdom from her own parents, she lacked a practical understanding of how to effectively relate to children, how to nurture affection. But she thought she knew.

'Wisdom' from Mom

So, Mom was always *there*, if only sometimes at church and ball games, and always dispensing advice, if with platitudes that had stopped being relevant in the 1930s, if they ever were.

She taught me how to give myself a manicure, for example, on her arbitrary theory that, "Fingernails are the first thing girls look at in young men." And we Snedeker boys were taught to open *all* doors for *all* females because, "Girls like to feel like that the man is in charge and taking care of them." Dad did it, too, we noticed, so we figured it must be all right.

Not until college, in the so-called radical feminist era in the late 1960s and '70s, did the lie rudely reveal itself to me. As I chivalrously, automatically, opened the passenger-side car door for a date one day, she said, much annoyed, "What are you doing *that* for? You think I can't open my own door?" Suddenly, I realized a *zeitgeist* change had occurred, probably decades, perhaps centuries, before, but guys had apparently failed to notice. For some reason, I never got the memo. Once I figured it out, though, I saved quite a lot of time *not* opening doors or pushing in chairs.

No matter. Mom still existed, early-twentieth-century notions still populating her consciousness, likely partly the result of sitting at one end of a narrow mahogany dining table as long as a bowling lane opposite Auntie Vava, her fabulously wealthy great aunt, as the noble dame quietly spooned her soup at the other end. A servant served them, walking the table briskly end to end.

MOMMY DEAREST

My mother's mother (Mama Frances to us kids) frequently dispatched little Betty off to Auntie Vava's San Francisco mansion to free up time for tennis or whatever self-gratifying activities her five-husband flightiness compelled. Auntie Vava's late husband had apparently prospered spectacularly in the medical-supplies business before he died, and his millions helped finance a privileged lifestyle for Mama Frances during my mother's early childhood.

But money ran like water through grandmother's fingers, and, when Auntie Vava died and left only an illiquid trust fund for her and my mother, Mama Frances quickly rendered herself and her daughter effectively penniless. She sold the quaint, charming hillside dream-home bequeathed to her by her generous aunt and tore through the profits of that, too. Thus, her privileged life—and that of my mother—quickly became a gilded conceit.

But, Mom, already steeped in the trappings of wealth, passed

30

through adolescence honoring the same upper-class assumptions. This in spite of the fact that her life with her mother during high school and after she married Dad more closely resembled modest middle class.

Unfortunately, she also knew that her mother, despite her sparkling gaiety and spectacularly green thumb, lacked essential character. And drank. A lot. Mom said she hesitated to bring her friends home after class in high school, fearful of finding her mother already well-toasted by mid-afternoon. Her father—Grandpa Brown to us—was a remote, granite-souled person, a vault of dark secrets (of which she became aware only many years later).

Mom grew to be a very conflicted, complicated woman with vague yearnings for past grandeur, insecurities about her relatively meager present reality, unresolved rage against but instinctive loyalty to profoundly damaged parents, and a deep cynicism regarding humankind's essential honesty and reliability. Or so I sensed. But I know for sure she cherished her family, as fully as the demons in her damaged soul ravaged her.

Unfortunately, the fears, resentments and genetic flaws of parents often visit their children. I'm afraid the ghosts of my mother's terrors and suspicions may yet be drifting aimlessly about in the gloomy, echoey corridors of my own subconscious.

But I'm convinced my mother tried as hard as she was able to be a good and devoted Mom, though her models were idealized and flawed through no fault of her own. I felt she saw us kids—as I'm sure her mother and father saw Mom and her brother—as interesting but a bit of a nuisance.

For Mom, cleaning house, planning a party or "having coffee" with neighbors was always more compelling than spending playful time with us. She simply had no idea how to play; it was a foreign country to her, an alien tongue, a charade. The constant noise, emotional and intellectual chaos, and free-ranging creativity of children just seemed too disruptive to her need for order, eternal "truths" and reassuring routines.

THE FAMILY HISTORIAN

Yet, despite her sometimes-awkward maternal instincts, she definitely loved family lore, on both sides of the clan. She served as the essential keeper of the flame of our history, all the way back to a Dutchman named Jan Snedeker who stepped off an immigrant boat in New Amsterdam, now New York, in 1632.

The apparently enterprising Jan later founded the community of Flatbush in New York City's Brooklyn borough. People today may associate it with the teen-gang movie, *The Lords of Flatbush*, starring, among others, Henry Winkler and Sylvester Stallone (a.k.a. later as "The Fonz" and "Rocky Balboa," respectively).

Much of the mental imagery of my childhood evolved from stories spun countless times by my mother, often during and immediately after meals as we chatted around the dining table. Now, it all feels like actual memory, the real and merely relayed conjoined. They were lovely stories, such as when twenty-one-year-old Dad, ever the teaser, proposed to my Mom during a short leave from World War II. In his deadpan, offhand way, Mom recalled, Dad suggested, "You *know*, Betty, we oughta get married." She was wary. They had been good friends since high school, often double-dating with others (she dated Dad's brother for a while and was best friends with a girl Dad long dated). They had for years known each other in a brother-sister, incest-taboo way. So, she instinctively replied, "You better be careful, Al. Someday some girl's going to take you *seriously*."

But, that's the thing; he *was* serious. My oh-so-traditional parents then quickly got married in of all places ... Tijuana, Mexico, where the transaction could be accomplished quicker. I love that—*Tijuana!*—then the capital of everything illicit, illegal and depraved. All of Dad's Navy unit attended the wedding. The morning after, every sailor in Dad's Navy unit lined both sides of the hotel stairway, parade swords aloft, cheering lustily as the newly christened married couple descended for breakfast like deer caught in headlights. My mother, still a committed virgin only a few short hours before (really, she said so), admitted she felt partly bemused and partly mortified at the time, blushing the color of, I'm guessing, a maraschino cherry.

Mom also told moving, poignant stories, such as ones involving her beloved only sibling, Uncle Jimmy—his first name, James, is my middle one—who died (valiantly, actually) in the brutal, tragic American assault on the Japanese stronghold at Iwo Jima during the war. The letter to Mama Frances from Uncle Jimmy's Army commander reported that he died heroically in a torrent of machine-gun fire as he tried to draw enemy gunfire away from his platoon's riflemen.

Mom idolized her brother, and I'm sure his passing only worsened her already implacable wariness of life: "This is not *fair!*" His pictures reveal a handsome, often smirking fellow with dark, thick, kinky hair (he wore a silk stocking to bed over his hair so it wouldn't be too bushy in the morning). I think of him in college pictures nattily dressed in a white tuxedo, ready for a party, always smiling brightly, his bushy hair somewhat compressed, the picture of privileged leisure. A young Great Gatsby. There's a snapshot taken of him by a girlhood friend of Mom's that I find particularly poignant, as he stands in his Army officer's uniform like a chivalrous knight, in Grandma Frances' verdant yard, with Mom's arms wrapped around him, her head leaning against his chest, a sweet, happy grin on her face.

Their mom and dad, as always, were elsewhere.

THE SADDEST STORY IN THE WORLD

The saddest story Mom ever told involved her rich Auntie Vava's butler, whose name I cannot recall.

The butler, also the great lady's chauffer, also served as a surrogate parent to my mother when she was young, taking her to motion-picture shows in San Francisco when she visited the mansion. She told us her best memories of childhood star that kindly butler, whom she loved with the warm-hearted devotion most people generally feel for parents or grandparents, or a particularly kindly uncle or aunt.

"He was *so* good to me," she told me more than once. "He talked to me, listened to me and bought me ice cream after every film. I was very fond of him."

But "very fond" vastly understated the reality, I suspect. In her many stories about the butler, I always sensed the visceral grief she suffered when he painfully disappeared without explanation one day in the rarely explained serial chaos and indifference that defined her childhood.

A BETTER MOTHER

When my mother died at eighty-eight, it saddened me, but I fear less than it should have.

Unfortunately, Mom and I were nearly identical in some ways; both of us were often remote, I think, from some of the essential little connections that naturally tie people to others, that draw us all together and ignite a longing, a constant pull, to stay attached. We seemed to resent the stand-offish quality we shared when we saw it in each other. We were selfish.

Ironically, the qualities she and Dad worked so hard to instill in us kids—self-reliance, self-sufficiency and common sense—were often wanting in her, although she always saw herself as a natural expert at life. Not to my credit, I could never quite tolerate this apparent deficiency in self-awareness. But disappointments in life, though often bitterly cold and regrettable, can also be inevitable. I wish I had been more capable of transcending them gracefully.

Yet I had enormous empathy in my heart for the cruel neglect my mother endured at the hands of her extraordinarily self-absorbed parents, and compassion for how it stunted her capacities to nurture love and connection in others and obtain it for herself. Even as Mama Freances lay dying, she unloaded an anvil of guilt on my blameless mother for not "being a better daughter." This kind of assault, one that erodes the spirit while the body lives, greatly wounded my mother. What hypocrisy.

One lesson I learned from my mother is that the value of family stories is mined less from their history than what they reveal about our heart of hearts. Her stories helped shape the soul of our family—the nexus of all of its fears, yearnings, triumphs, joys and failures over the years. These stories immortalized us in a sense, cultivating in each subsequent generation knowledge of the lives of all the others of our tribe who came before.

In the end, nearly deaf, going blind from macular degeneration, barely mobile and slowly being ravaged by emphysema and congestive heart failure, Mom believed, correctly, that her life had already effectively ended. "I'm ready to die," she said matter-of-factly more than once. Physically unable to enjoy music, reading, movies or even conversation—the essential beloved entertainments of her long life—she didn't see the point anymore. She told me her existence had sharply narrowed to simply waiting for the end, and she deeply resented not being able to control her own *denouement*. But nothing could be done about it. No "death with dignity" laws existed in Arizona, like those in Oregon and now California. No way to quicken the pace, if she so chose. In her eyes, the deficit exposed just one more instance of life's inherent unfairness. It's random, careless, malignant insults.

Happily, her stories remain. Besides keeping the history of our family alive over generations, the tales she so joyously, proudly told also illuminated all of the most beautiful and elegant qualities of the wounded teller. I must admit that despite all her imperfections, most far beyond her own responsibility, she proved a far better mother than I was a son.

I probably underestimated her to the end. But, in fact, she was like Shakespeare's *MacBeth*, a play whose memorable phrases became so seamlessly embedded in the English language that they are now almost universal clichés. "What's done is done," sayeth Lady MacBeth. "Life is short," saidith Mom.

Ironically, my mother's life proved far longer than she wished. But I tend to honor the shortness of existence she alluded to, treasuring each day as though it were my last, with nary a thought it one day might drag mercilessly on—as it did for my mom—torturing me and everyone around me to the end.

Kindly Auntie Vava.

Uncle Jimmy and Aunt Barb.

"Cheesecake" for husbands at war.

Mom and Jim during the war.

Mother and daughter.

Mom as a little girl. Adorable.

Mom and Dad's wedding day.

Next to Dhahran tennis courts.

Affectionate Mike and bratty me.

CHAPTER 5

MIKE

MY BIG BROTHER. Literally and figuratively.

As a young boy I looked up to him, far more than he wanted, and I obsessed about hanging out with him and his friends, although they were about six years older. Perhaps *because* they were six years older. I was the stereotypical pesky kid brother, whom Mike and his friends probably wished would just vanish.

I remember, at maybe five or six, following him and a group of buddies as they left our house to go do something I imagined would be adventurous. My brother stopped, looked back sharply at me and said, "You can't come." I tried to insist, was rebuffed again and quite possibly a third time, finally standing there glumly as the gang of boys faded into the distance.

HONUS WAGNER

I once had a Honus Wagner baseball card as a youth and thinking of that card reminds me of my brother. Wagner, a legendary shortstop, was an awkward-seeming farm boy when he joined the Pittsburgh Pirates of the professional National League, but once he took the field he transformed into a gazelle.

My brother was a lanky, pale, awkward-looking redhead always far taller than his classmates, even towering over some of his coaches. But under a shambling exterior, Mike possessed a natural athlete's grace. Once on the baseball diamond or basketball court, appearances of clumsiness disappeared, replaced by a fluid agility. In Little League and Pony League baseball, he dominated as a fastball pitcher and exhibited a sharp-eyed knack for laying his bat cleanly on the ball.

At Notre Dame International, the Catholic boys' boarding high school he attended in Rome, Italy, he starred as a hook-shooting forward on the varsity basketball team when it won the European championship in 1962. His team played in a league comprised mostly of squads from American military bases in Europe and Turkey, which allowed players to compete in exciting international cities. Emulating and envying Mike, I played Little League and American Legion baseball, and varsity basketball at McClintock High School in Tempe, Arizona, 1966-68. I was always a credible athlete but never a breakaway star or a champion, as he was.

By following in Mike's footsteps, I thoroughly enjoyed the overwhelming thrills of sport and even some brief, fleeting moments of glory on fields and courts of boyhood dreams. I wouldn't trade any of it. Possibly to my father's disappointment (though he never showed it), neither of his boys ended up playing college ball, as he had.

But the athletic genes we surely inherited from him (Mom clearly had none) bequeathed to us the joy and the confidence of belonging during tentative adolescence, which I'm sure pleased him. I'm also certain that what he mainly cared about was that we turned out to be happy, productive men who tried to make the world better by not making it worse.

MY FAVORITE PHOTO

When Mike appears in my memories of Saudi Arabia, it's always in a horizontal-striped T-shirt, rolled-up jeans and Keds, his carrot-top hair sticking straight up in a kind of tall flat-top, his own tallness star-tling. He always had a look of absolute innocence, as though if someone said a bad word he would be shocked. But he was a good kid and kindly, even to me, the pesky kid brother.

One of my favorite pictures from childhood (the one that opens this chapter) leans against the wall today on a picture rail in the master bedroom, showing Mike, about ten, sitting on a chair, hugging an unco-operative me, about four. I seem to have been walking by minding my own business when my naturally affectionate brother grabbed me for a quick hug. At a glance, it shows our different temperaments—his, kind-hearted and warm; mine, detached, remote, focused somewhere else. I didn't know it at the time, but I truly needed the recurrent, genuine con-nections he provided.

He never held my natural apart-ness against me, as far as I could tell. I only remember his ever really getting mad at me once, and it involved an enormous box of baseball cards. And, yes, I had it coming. But more on the fateful baseball-card incident later. Aside from that, though, Mike was congenitally charitable and honorable as a youngster, and he is exactly the same today. Some say our basic characters coalesce by the time we reach four. Seems absolutely true for my big brother. He's always been this way.

From age seven until I left Saudi Arabia at eleven, in 1962, Mike was away at school in Rome. The difference in our ages and the trajectories of our lives meant we weren't really able to develop any kind of durable relationship until we were in our fourties and fifties. Added to our sep-arateness was that I spent a lot of years working abroad. And I did some selfish things that also probably didn't endear me to him; for instance, I once got a new job and immediately moved to a new town, leaving him high and dry and forced to quickly move from the suddenly too-expen-sive two-bedroom apartment we had been sharing.

GROWING TOGETHER

But I like to think all has been forgiven or diminished through the years. In any case, we now have that comfortable brotherly relationship that makes watching a baseball game together fun and, in some curious way, nurturing ("Jeez, where did those #%!?* bums learn to play *defense!*"). As older guys, I've discovered we both seem to prefer a similar laid-back, methodical cadence to our lives. Much to the occasional—*they* might say "frequent"—chagrin of our much-more-dynamic wives.

I've enjoyed watching my brother's two boys—Scott and Andy—grow into men and thinking of them as part of a Snedeker continuum, symbols of our family's persisting evolution. Both grew up into decent, caring guys, and I think that's a fine reflection on their dad that transcends any of the usual struggles all boys have with their fathers growing up. Scott has an oblique connection to Saudi Arabia, passing through the Middle East as a U.S. Army soldier during the first Gulf War in 1991, and Andy knows all the family stories from Arabia past, long repeated ad nauseum.

THE CONTENT OF CHARACTER

One of my brother's most admirable qualities is the complete and absolute absence of any bigotry in his nature.

He is one of those rare people who really is class- and color-blind, seeing people wholly by the content of their character, not the color of their skin or glitter of their status. As far as I've ever been able to detect, if you treat other people well, you're always okay in my brother's book. His optimistic faith in humankind beats my congenital cynicism any day of the week.

Being able to play sports with my brother after we became adults provided one of the joys of my life. When we were both living in the Phoenix area in the 1970s, we played together on a city league basketball team. The team didn't do so hot, but we had never before played on the same squad, and to me it still felt like winning, like recapturing something great we never had to begin with. Sometime later, we bowled together in a co-ed league with a couple of female co-workers from his company; I enjoyed watching again his graceful, fluid athleticism that I remembered from our boyhood. A bonus: our team won the league championship.

It's funny how the number of years between people seems to decrease over time until it's as if you could actually have been born on the same day. Mike is now in his mid-seventies and retired from a career of many years in the electronics manufacturing industry he entered after graduating from Arizona State University with a business degree. He and his wife, Denise, live a quiet life in an Arizona suburb, enjoying their leisure, children and grandchildren. My wife and I live in the Midwest heartland, regularly flying to Arizona to visit them, as they visit us on our quiet, gently flowing creek.

One of my favorite boyhood images of my brother is a baseball team photo of him with his Bruins teammates in the Dhahran Pony League. He is smiling broadly, joyfully in his sharp red-and-gray uniform with "DHAHRAN" stitched upper-case across the chest in vivid red, a preternaturally buoyant kid. It's a gift.

A STAND-UP GUY

But, still, he was no pushover.

I remember a story about when as a freshman at Rome's Notre Dame International Catholic high school, Mike was cruelly taunted by a classmate about his new hearing aids. My brother refused to wilt under the disrespect, directly challenging the bully. Noticing the conflict, one of the Congregation of the Holy Cross brothers at the school directed the two boys to don boxing gloves and resolve the matter with fisticuffs in the gym. Mike whipped his—suddenly former—tormentor's posterior.

Years later in another incident, Mike was at a party where two guys began throwing punches. Ever the peacemaker, my brother stepped between them—and caught a haymaker in the lip. The next day, he displayed the most grotesquely swollen, colorful injury I had ever seen, his lip so hideously inflated with swelling, I scarcely recognized him.

But he would have done it again before lunch without a thought.

By the way, the kid Mike whipped in Rome later became one of his best friends. That's also my big brother.

With good pal Janet Fleharty before a dance.

Mike and I in front yard.

Proud letterman with Grandma Dolly in Hong Kong.

Mike and wife, Denise, early on.

Nearly as tall as his Little League coaches.

"The Beav" wasn't any wholesomer.

STUDENT-FACULTY Basketball game where the faculty outplayed the students 36–22 shows Henry Pappas, (faculty) moving in aggressively against Mike Snedeker (left) and Dave Wasson.

Immortalized in the *Sun and Flare*.

Son Scott in Kuwait during Desert Storm I.

The sweetest little girl in the world.

CHAPTER 6
KATHY

SHE WAS THE cutest, sweetest, pink-cheeked little girl you can imagine. Golden, strawberry-blonde hair, a creamy complexion and a shy, adorably unpretentious smile.

But Kathleen, whom we all called "Kathy" or just "Kath," surprised as well. In one classic Snedeker home movie she is wearing a short, ruffled sun dress, at about age three. Just as she gets to the cameraman (Dad), she squints bashfully into the bright sunlight and suddenly raises the skirt over her head, revealing her scrawny, little-girl body beneath. Spontaneous and completely out of character, simultaneously.

Kathy is about sixteen months older than I am, but we weren't really as inseparable as brothers and sisters that close in age often are, although we generally got along well. On those *rare* occasions we didn't, however (I readily assume fault owing to my far more aggressive nature), Mom's punishment for such sibling conflict was extreme: I was forced to play dolls with Kathy all afternoon. How I survived that only slightly damaged, I'll never know.

DEATH'S DOOR

Kathy caught the measles when she was about eight or nine, and I was six or seven. At the time measles was ravaging the kids in Dhahran, spreading like wildfire. After being infected and symptoms first appeared, neither Kathy nor I felt the least bit sick. For a couple of days we both ran around the house, feeling fine, extraordinarily proud of our little red spots.

But then something terrible happened.

One morning, I saw Kathy lying on her back in her bed, Mom sitting beside her, with a hard, furrowed expression. From her bedroom doorway I noticed, with alarm, that Kathy's normally pale face now appeared beet red and puffy, starkly framed by the white pillow behind her head. Her eyes were closed; she looked asleep—but in reality (I know now) she was knocking on "death's door."

Shortly thereafter, Mom and Dad took her to the hospital in Dhahran, and I didn't get to see her again for what seemed like weeks; I wasn't allowed to visit her at the hospital for fear one or both of us would be at risk. I didn't understand my banishment at the time, and I certainly didn't comprehend the full gravity of the situation. My sister had developed acute *encephalitis*, a dangerous if not common brain complication of measles, and had fallen into a deep coma. The doctors warned my parents to prepare for the worst, for the reality that she *very likely* might die. And even if she did survive, they cautioned, she probably would have significant residual brain damage.

Kathy remained quarantined in the hospital, without any visits from her siblings. Even so, one of my brother's classmates said he had heard that Kathy would be "crazy" if she ever came home at all, frightening gentle-hearted Mike half to death. He *loved* his sister, like he loved everybody, but even more so. Eventually he got to visit her, though my personal ban remained in full effect. (In my experience, I never got to do anything, especially if everybody else got to.)

Kathy remained in a coma for more than a week, with nurses and doctors keeping constant vigil. But one night, out of nowhere, she simply woke up, uttering these glorious words: "I have to go to the bathroom." Soon, she resumed speaking and behaving normally—not like some "crazy" person—but the doctors still counseled my parents that the shock to her brain would likely render her far more emotionally fragile and erratic than they remembered, at least for a while.

Mom and Dad went to see Kathy after she awoke from what they described to me as a long "sleep." They brought Mike with them to relieve his growing anxiety. The cute little redheaded girl, confounding everyone, had lived. Not only lived, but seemed to come out of the deep, dark woods pretty much her old self.

When Mike saw his now-alert and smiling sister, Mom said he took her hand and cried. As did my folks and Kathy's primary doctors and nurses, who were present as well, and everyone else within a hundred feet. I'm sure I would have, too, if invited.

Kathy recovered completely, compounding the extreme nature of her seeming miracle. As forewarned, she behaved a little squirrely at first as the wiring in her brain's emotional control center settled down after the fevered short-circuit. But it wasn't long before she resumed being the same sweetheart she always was, playing with her friends, being nice to undeserving me, studying ballet.

THE FUNNIEST BALLET MOVIE EVER

A ballet classic in the Snedeker home movie collection stars a maybe six-year-old Kathy. In it, she shows off her ballet "skills" against a white sheet backdrop that Dad set up to make the film look arty.

Well, whatever that video is, it isn't arty. Right of the bat in the film, Kathy slightly pulled a groin muscle doing a kick and had to sit down and rub it and make pained faces, with film rolling. Then she bent over into a backbend with her hands flat on the floor, an impressive achievement. But her slick-slippered feet immediately started verrrrry slowwwwwwly sliding out from under her. We *knew* what would happen! As anticipated, her feet finally shot straight, and she slammed into the floor. In a final ballet scene, she crouched on all fours and kicked one leg upward so that the sole of her foot—at least theoretically—would gently tap her head. However, executed far more energetically than necessary, the gentle *tap-tap-tap* morphed into a vigorous self-pummeling—WHAP! WHAP! WHAP!

BATH WITH KATH

Nightly bath time was another form of entertainment for Kathy and me, at least for a while.

The nightly ritual included a great froth of detergent bubbles, floating duckies and other toys, and, of course, a whole lot of bathroom-drenching splashing around while Mom incessantly shouted, "Stop that this instant!" Sometimes I would submerge under the bubbles and hold my breath, while Mom fearfully and fruitlessly kept sticking her hand in trying to locate me under a cloud of Tide foam while I dodged her from the deep.

Then one watershed night, when Kathy was about eight, Mom announced that henceforth and forevermore we would be bathed *separately*. What?! I *liked* bath-time with Kath. But, in this case what I wanted didn't count. Mom briefly explained that Kathy was "maturing," and that was that.

Kathy and I shared a Volkswagen bug in college, and she ultimately became a nurse—including in an emergency room!—married an engineer named Joe (who was once drafted by a pro baseball team and is as handy as I am not), and together they had three great kids, two of them redheads. They just welcomed their second grandchild not long ago and continue to mull what their retirement (already underway) will actually involve.

Kathy has had the great good fortune of being able to live her life as though she had never suffered a coma at all.

Rocking a hobo.

Kathy and husband, Joe Watts.

With neighbor girls in front yard.

Our moms join us at school.

The happy Snedeker kids.

Whose birthday is it?

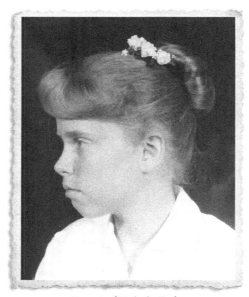

Portrait of Kathy by Dad.

The budding ballerina.

Grandma Dolly was playful but physically commanding.

GRANDMA DOLLY

WHEN MY MOSTLY Germanic grandmother Dolly, my dad's mom, was 61, she decided to spend $6,000 of her "filthy lucre" (she also had some Scots-Irish) to come visit us in Dhahran. "You can't take it with you," she always said, earth money not being any good in heaven, as I vaguely understood it.

'WELCOME' TO ARABIA

Grandma's visit to the desert started out poorly.

Customs at Dhahran Airport at the time consisted of a long, single-file string of narrow portable tables under an awning next to the runway. For some reason the customs guys decided to tear through the suitcase of my very dignified Grandma as if she were a whiskey smuggler or, worse, an apostate. They pulled out her underpants and bras, which to me seemed alarmingly huge at the time, and held them up for all to fully appreciate, while Grandma's neck got redder and redder and her clenched-jaw muscles tighter and tighter. They finally let her go, but she was steamed.

Once at our house, she hadn't been inside more than ten minutes when she shut the refrigerator door on our cat Snowball's tail, instantly making her his permanent arch-enemy. From then on, whenever Grandma came down the hall, Snowball would back v-e-r-y s-l-o-w-l-y out of it, never taking his eyes off her, and then disappear under the nearest bed.

SIDIQI AND SILLY HATS

But things got better for Grandma. She went to a neighborhood party one night where everyone wore weird hats; Grandma's had a bird on top (I've seen pictures). She had fun and drank quite a lot of sidiqi, I was told.

She stayed three months in Dhahran and then joined us on our planned ninety-day 'round-the-world long vacation to the States, where we left her at her home in California. On that trip, I got a whole room to myself in a Hong Kong hotel suite because, it turned out, Grandma suffered claustrophobia in the little, windowless room my folks reserved for her to give her privacy. No way, she decided, opting for a room with my sister instead. I inherited hers, which I loved.

Grandmother Dolly—we called her, more informally, Grandma, which she hated—was one of my favorite people in the world. And I could tell I was one of hers, too.

'BEDROOM EYES'

Grandma used to tell me, as a kid, that I had "bedroom eyes," but the meaning escaped me until I was grown and realized Grandma was maybe a little bit saucier in real life than I had imagined.

The proof became evident on her deathbed, after cervical cancer had whittled her once stately and commanding presence down to about ninety-five pounds. "Always remember," she advised me, with surprising vigor and urgency as I hugged her for what turned out to be the last time, "the government's got you by the balls."

I know. My ears burned, too.

As grandmother lay dying I remembered a poignant story my dad's sister, Aunt Kela, once told me years before. Kela said she had been outside the room one day where her father lay dying, and she could hear her mother and him talking quietly inside. "My father said, 'You've been a good wife to me,'" she recalled, still moved by the memory.

In those patriarchal days, it was a supreme, even affective compliment, but I can only guess how my highly independent grandmother felt about it.

Grandma at Dhahran bird-hat party.

Enjoying Mrs. Hammond's birdcage hat.

Working woman, circa 1940s.

Grandma, left, and her strong-willed sisters.

With Grandpa Father not long before he died.

Grandma and Aunt Helen (later
Sabrina) elegantly attired.

Dolly and kids, Kela and Frank, during WWII.

Dhahran community parade, 1950s.

CHAPTER 8
OASIS

AMID EAST-COAST SAUDI Arabia's desolate terrain, Dhahran, barely two or three miles square, stood out, a green exclamation in the endless tan.

Even by the early 1950s, Dhahran's camp forest of imported, multinational trees had grown large and leafy, throwing a broad relief of shade over the community. With its wide, verdant streets and tidy rows of simple, rectangular, ranch-style houses, green with hedges and other foliage, the camp resembled a well-watered, lower-middle-class suburb in Arizona or Texas, where in fact many of the early oilmen had come from.

The only sign anything might not be completely benign was a twelve-foot-high, chain-link fence that encircled the town of 4,500 or so souls and guarded its gates. Only those with an Aramco badge were allowed to enter. But in truth it didn't really occur to us that the fences and guards might indicate potential danger. They just became a normal part of the landscape, like the bright red Aramco company vehicles with white Arabic and English numbers on the side. Once you entered the sanctified interior of our little town, all serious worries and unpleasantness seemed perpetually marooned outside. On the Dhahran side of the fence, a modest utopian paradise thrived.

We lived in comfortable if plain duplexes and detached single-story, single-family homes. Company-supplied residential furniture was typically mid-century style—clean, spare, and blonde. The living was easy in Dhahran in the early days.

TELEVISION!

Then, in 1958 Aramco TV began broadcasting and families began to cluster around their little television sets to watch *Ozzie and Harriet*, *Perry Mason*, *Father Knows Best*, *I Love Lucy*, *Gunsmoke* and *Superman*. During the four or so hours of daily TV broadcast, we were also treated to professional baseball and even wrestling with Gorgeous George. The U.S. Air Force base near al-Khobar added fifteen minutes of nightly broadcast with a news show at 9:45. As I recall, the anchor was a uniformed, deadpan airman reading from an *Associated Press* script. It bored us silly as kids, of course, but if we convinced Mom and Dad we actually *wanted* to watch the news, they allowed us to stay up until the program ended at 10. Having a chance to stay up past our embarrassingly early bedtime was as exciting as having our three-riyal (ninety-cent) weekly allowance tripled, so we went for it as often as we could.

Most nights the Snedeker kids had to hit the sack by the ungodly early hour of nine. All the kids in the neighborhood knew it, and my friends with later curfews—which is to say *all* of them—would often rap outside my bedroom window to pester me. Happily, for a glorious month or two in summer, when the sun didn't sink below the horizon until 9:30 or so, our parents graciously extended bedtime, allowing us extra daylight with our friends.

UTOPIA

Unless your parents enforced a depressingly early bedtime, kids had little or no stress in Dhahran.

The camp provided everything a normal, aggressively self-centered youngster might need or desire. It also represented a kind of utopia for the adults, as well. Dhahran was the company town to end all company towns, totally unlike the blue-collar lifestyle immortalized by Tennessee Ernie Ford in the song, "Sixteen Tons." Rather than like his immortal words, "another day older and deeper in debt," in Dhahran, it was more like, "another day older and happier yet!"

In comfortable, well-equipped bungalows for families and cozy pre-fab apartments for singles, air conditioning was essential. Indeed, with outside temperatures routinely flirting with 120 degrees, any tolerable quality of life required AC. Indeed, AC was so omnipresent its icy chill instantly evaporated any sweat when you entered any building, and, conversely, you were immediately flash-broiled and drenched in sweat when you stepped outside, especially in humidity-drenched August.

One quirky Dhahran reality: All home kitchens had two water faucets, one for "raw" hard water used in cleaning, flushing and bathing, and one for "sweet" water purged of salt and other minerals for drinking. And only one bathroom, no matter how many kids you had.

At first, we took maximum advantage of the dirt-cheap local domestic services available: houseboys, gardeners, and drivers. A few were Muslim Arabs, but for the most part these jobs were filled by Christian Indians (from India). Having so much domestic help added to the languorous colonial vibe that lulled Dhahran into somnolence despite the reluctance of equality-conscious Americans to think of themselves as colonial overlords. We kids certainly didn't sense any white supremacist edge to life in Dhahran. Everybody got along fine as far as we could tell, although the "help" clearly had no authority. Adults treated the houseboys in a mostly kindly fashion but as children requiring constant direction.

The ragged, soiled, aromatic gardeners often fetched discarded shoes from our garbage that they were later seen wearing. Because Americans had much bigger feet, this was immediately obvious by the toes that curled up and flopped like clown shoes as their new owners walked in them. Sadly, the glaring inequities of that time and place seemed perfectly natural to us kids.

DOMESTICS

The houseboys were a spic-and-span lot.

I remember their looking like mental-ward orderlies in the movie *One Flew Over the Cuckoo's Nest*, stark in their spotlessly white shirts and pants. Many of these workers were from India's sun-baked tropical southern regions, such as Goa, their skin a black sun-baked hue that contrasted sharply with the vivid white of their eyes and meticulously bleached clothes.

The domestics lived just outside the main community in a cramped, slapdash shantytown of corrugated tin dwellings called *barastis* (pronounced ba-RASS-tees). Named after simple Saudi traditional village structures made of palm fronds and thatch, they were in reality far less charming. Years later, when the woefully substandard barastis became an embarrassment to the government, Aramco demolished and replaced them with improved housing, although the new barracks were not plush by any stretch.

Despite their dismal accommodations, the Indian camp workers I knew were cheerful, industrious, orderly men invariably kind to children. I am told some weren't, but that was never my personal experience.

GARDENS AND GARDENERS

The local gardeners were generally Arabs—mostly Yemenis. The landscaping workers seemed very poor to me, dressed in tattered, dingy khakis and grimy white headscarves swirled and tucked about their skulls in a careless, haphazard fashion.

Gardeners in our neighborhood brought their lunch every day in identical circular, stackable aluminum containers about five inches in diameter and an inch deep. A vertical metal band secured the stack for carrying and also served as a handle at the top. Each container enclosed a particular dish, such as rice, unleavened flat bread, meat and vegetables. I thought it an impressively efficient apparatus. At lunchtime, the workers would sit in a circle facing one another under a tree, unstacking and fanning their personal array of containers out on the ground, like Vegas dealers.

We kids were transfixed by the gardeners' prayer rituals. As Muslims, they all prayed the prescribed five times a day, repeatedly standing and muttering alien words with their palms turned upward, then kneeling and pressing their foreheads into our thick lawns before rising to repeat the same ritual again. As they prayed, we would stand close, curious and watchful, which they generally ignored. A few barked words in Arabic we didn't understand—*Ka-LAHS!* (Enough!), *YALL-a!* (Hurry up! Come on!)—but with enough volume and vigor that their meaning was crystal clear: Stop that! NOW! Go away!

The results of the lowly gardeners' labors were astonishing. From its early days, Dhahran exuded an Eden-in-the-desert quality, thanks to the ceaseless efforts of these faceless workers. The community's foliage blended exotic with mundane, a rainbow profusion of plants from Egypt, Jordan, Lebanon, Africa, India, and other foreign locales. A teeming variety of trees loomed everywhere: massive, thick-trunked behemoths, such as Indian banyans and Peepuls, rarely seen in America; slender ones with flat, shallow parasol crowns, like acacias, flame trees, and the aptly named "umbrella trees" common to African savannas; squat date palms and slim, towering palms of other, non-date species; the white-flowered, perfumed frangipani, whose large, oar-shaped leaves drop annually; and finally, the hardy eucalyptus, or gum trees. The long roots of the eucalyptus plunged deep into the earth, often insinuating themselves destructively around and through underground utility pipes.

Flowering plants vividly colored the community's palette. My dad lovingly planted scarlet hibiscus in our yard; other common blooms were yellow elder; lavender arborea; fifteen-foot-tall oleanders with pink leaves; China rose; vermillion bougainvillea; the fire-hued bird-of-paradise; purple *glabra* from Italy; red, wine, pink, salmon or orange *spectabilis* from India; red pomegranate; and multi-colored periwinkles, pansies, petunias, geraniums, and daisies.

Throughout the community, miles and miles of jasmine hedges bordered residential yards. When first planted, they looked like sticks, but they rapidly grew into densely green and nearly indestructible hedge rows. As a kid, I marveled about how these inert-looking "sticks" came alive and quickly circumscribed every house in the neighborhood.

The water for all this floral abundance came from ancient, non-renewable, subterranean aquifers far below the arid desert. So once consumed, these precious potable elixirs disappeared. Decades later, burgeoning water demand for the fast-growing Saudi Arab populace forced the government to consider supplemental sources. Massive desalination plants suddenly began popping up along the Gulf and Red Sea other either coast.

When I was a reporter in al-Khobar in the eighties, I covered the construction of a humongous desal plant on the Gulf. It reminded me of the massive but drab Third Reich-like structures in the desolate film *1984*. A South Korean company had won the contract, and a veritable army of Korean convicts (I was told) were imported by the contractor to supply labor.

Shrimp 'campi'

Pungent fishermen wearing colorful Yemeni-style wrap-around "skirts" or long, dingy white, Saudi-style tunics would regularly appear in our camp dragging four-foot-long woven sacks.

The bags brimmed with slithery masses of giant fresh gulf shrimp. The vendors would suddenly appear just outside our alley gate. My Mom walked out to them and typically bought a gallon's worth of prawns—"*Riyal khamsa, memsahib* ("Five riyals, madam"), they'd say. After the transaction, they'd drag their basket to the next house.

That evening, Mom would toss the jumbo prawns into a deep-fat fryer filled with boiling, crackling Crisco purchased at the commissary. Once crisped and then sprinkled with fresh lemon juice, the fried shrimp was heaven in your mouth. On occasion, the fish vendors also brought enormous, surprisingly heavy fillets of butt-ugly but delicious *hamour*, a bottom-dwelling flat fish with eyes atop the head, mild-tasting flesh, and many hidden bones. Certainly, other fish also thrived in the gulf, but, for some reason, we ate only shrimp and hamour.

Yet, it wasn't all fun and games in utopia.

Mom and Dad on New Year's Eve.

Hobby Farm offered equestrian recreation. (Courtesy Saudi Aramco)

Community was lush by mid-century.
(Courtesy Saudi Aramco)

Dhahran youth jitterbug at the school.
(Courtesy Saudi Aramco)

Bedouin and his donkey caddy for golfers at Dhahran Rolling Hills Golf Course.
(Courtesy Saudi Aramco)

Families gather for fun
at Half Moon Bay.

Kids could choose swimming or tennis. (Courtesy Saudi Aramco)

Gardening at home. (Courtesy Saudi Aramco)

The way it was: Steve and I in alley behind 4491-B.

Chapter 9
4491-B

4491-B. Our house.

Ours was one among twelve identical and nondescript single-story dwellings in two linear strings of six duplexes each directly facing each other in our immediate neighborhood, like opposing armies in a battlefield diagram.

Confusingly, our so-called "back" yards were tiny and faced one another across a once-sand but later asphalt-paved alleyway, our neighborhood's primary social thoroughfare. The opposite "front" yards, much larger and enclosed by high walls, faced the front walls of another string of duplexes on the other side of a concrete walkway.

I have no idea who determined which were "front" and which "back," or why. But it always seemed to me that the entrance you most used should be the "front," and the entrance less used the "back." But logic wasn't part of it, apparently.

Nonetheless, many of my most vivid childhood memories involve that house and that alleyway.

THE NEIGHBORHOOD

Each house was roofed in colorless corrugated steel and clad in faint gray-green siding, with a tiny hedge-lined yard opening to the alley and a larger, enclosed private space on the opposite side of the house that opened onto a sidewalk.

The larger yard covered about nine hundred square feet and was surrounded by seven-foot cement-block walls that converged on an enclosed, wood-slatted entry atrium with a fifteen-foot-tall roof and patio access up several steps. Like high-walled traditional Saudi dwellings that frustrated prying eyes, our backyard sanctuaries assured a measure of privacy.

The neighborhood's shady, oasis-like "front" patios attracted an unending series of impromptu parties, where homemade hooch flowed freely. The net effect: a nearly continuous twinkling of laughter throughout the neighborhood in late afternoon and early evening.

I can still picture the adults chatting and chuckling amiably, standing around or sitting at a paint-peeling picnic table or in one of those '50s-style winged patio chairs (plain canvas covers stretched over a thin-tubed metal frame). The women often wore knee-length cotton shorts and sleeveless blouses in mild months (when parties flourished), with the dads, often just home from work, still in their corporate togs— slacks of thin, gently draping fabric, and short-sleeved, pale and plain cotton shirts. Casual, comfortable, contented. The Aramco way.

These inviting patios provided perfect escapes for the moveable feast of adult after-hours social entertainment in Dhahran neighborhoods.

COFFEE BREAKS

On the other hand, the small built-in breakfast nooks in Aramco kitchens provided the locus of morning and afternoon coffee breaks for neighborhood moms, all stay-at-homes because few Aramco jobs for women existed in camp in those years. Well-leisured by servants, moms had plenty of time and energy for coffee.

That meant on no-school days, weekdays or holidays, if we needed to find our mother we often had to reconnoiter *every single* kitchen table in the neighborhood until we found her. Inexplicably to us kids, they thought it funny we had to hunt them down.

THE NEIGHBORS

Over the years, my family's best friends in the neighborhood were, serially, the Williamsons, Heltons and Congletons.

The Williamsons were always our neighbors when we lived at 4491-B (others moved in and out of adjacent units over the years); our houses were side-by-side, the end units of two duplexes bisected by a narrow sidewalk. They were a nice family—devilishly handsome Joe Williamson, an Aramco pilot, his sexily pretty wife, Barbara, and their kids, Joe, Danny and adorable towheaded baby Susie. Danny, a year or so older than me, was my constant tormentor.

Catty-corner from us, just southwest of where the adjacent side and "front" sidewalks intersected, lived the Heltons: parents Joe and Betty, gregarious, black-haired Texans, and about five kids, of whom Steve was my best pal.

When the Heltons left, the Congletons moved into their unit: dad Bert, a rugged-looking but dapper fellow who I remember sipping highballs, tossing darts and relaxing in their front yard during balmy evenings; his wife, Aggie, a tall elegant woman who seemed somewhat detached and ethereal; and their kids—sensitive, towheaded Jimmy who became a good friend of mine, and gentle, timid Cherie, a tiny, fragile-looking girl who reminded me of a baby sparrow.

I only vaguely remember those who lived in the other houses, including the Ramirez's, Heisings, and Whitters (one of whose sons once, sleepwalking, rang every doorbell in the neighborhood at 2 a.m.), the Blauvelts and Duels (whose daughter, Gail, was nicknamed "Stormy"), and the Pedersons. Mr. Pederson, head of Aramco's Safety Department, once received a departmental safety award with his foot in a cast—a remnant, Dad said, of his jumping unsafely off the diving board at Dhahran pool.

A Mrs. Southerland lived a couple houses up the alley from us but we never saw her except when she made chocolate-chip cookies and passed them out, still warm at her alley-side door.

I fondly remember the outdoor sleepovers Jimmy Congleton and I enjoyed at each other's houses on weekend nights, snug in our sleeping bags unfurled on the lawn. We would lie on the cool grass, gazing up at the black, desert sky unpolluted by big-city lights, mesmerized by the immaculate, twinkling cosmos above, and obsessively counting shooting stars. Zing. Zip. It felt like camping out, far beyond parents and rules, but with indoor toilets close by. The weather was often perfect for outdoor sleeping, too, especially in the late spring and fall—slightly cool with a gentle breeze at night. I can't remember a thing we talked about, except, "Whoa, there goes another one," as our eyes traced the long, shallow arc of another streaking comet. Soon, we'd be blissfully asleep.

SAND, SAND EVERYWHERE

By the mid-fifties, asphalt macadam had replaced sand in our alley, which meant that instead of everything inside our houses being covered with a half-inch of dust, barely a quarter-inch piled up daily thereafter.

One day, long after the asphalting, a few neighbors decided in tandem to wash down our alley and then they suddenly materialized in what we used to call "work clothes." They dragged lawn hoses into the alleyway and proceeded to spray it down—sweeping the muddy torrent down the gentle slope from 8th Street toward 3rd in a coordinated assault. Soon, practically everybody in the neighborhood had joined the activity, which, naturally, turned into a party. I recall one woman shouting vague protestations from her porch as though the neighborhood had gone completely mad, but everyone else was having so much fun they ignored her.

Odd as that day may have seemed to some, it also reflected normalcy.

In Dhahran, especially in the early days when amenities were more spartan, Aramcons often created their own excitement and entertainment. Fun in any form whatsoever was like found money.

And "fun" could be anything including clothes lines, which in our neighborhood graced alley-side yards whose waist-high hedges put everyone's laundry on display as it dried in the blistering sun. Thus, we all knew who wore boxers and "whitey tighties," who had enormous brassieres or unremarkable little ones, whose kids were bed-wetters and whose moms rarely laundered. You can learn a lot from a clothesline.

Privacy schmivacy

Regarding privacy, one mother up the alley was rumored to cook breakfast topless, for some unfathomable reason, and my dad joked that she probably had to be mighty careful not to inadvertently dip "something" in the popping bacon grease.

But my parents would never let me out of the house at breakfast time to validate the rumor. Sadly, this prohibition deprived me of important exposure (so to speak) that might have been critical to my developing appropriate adult cynicism that comes from learning whether or not people actually make stuff up all the time. If the alleged topless chef had simply put an opaque blind on her kitchen door, ensuring privacy, that horse would never have gotten out of the barn. But even in our own house in Dhahran, privacy was mostly an illusion.

One day my mother busily cleaned a toilet at the far end of the house, as the Grundig stereo in the living room boomed out the braying of Mario Lanza or some other operatic tenor. Neither Mom nor I heard or noticed when Mrs. Williamson, our next-door neighbor and close friend of Mom's, walked into the house. It was normal; in the quasi-commune atmosphere of the neighborhood, people were always walking into each other's houses, calling out, "Anybody home?" or "YOO-hoo!"

But on *that* day, we didn't hear her come in and she startled my mother when she finally found her back in the bathroom. Mom abruptly started screaming at the now also startled Mrs. Williamson about how she must "never, ever, under any circumstances, sneak up" on her again. Mrs. Williamson, a sweet, lively woman, quickly fled, and Mom calmly went back to scrubbing the bathroom as if nothing had happened. But I knew *something* had.

Looking back, I believe some obscure psychic wound, long scarred over, had been nicked.

THE GIRL UP THE ALLEY

I myself occasionally assaulted others' privacy, included the time I ratted out my brother to my parents for sneaking out the window of our shared bedroom to visit comely, dark-eyebrowed Gail Nickerson, his hoped-for girlfriend, who lived up the block. He insists he never did any such thing, that I probably dreamed it or, more likely, made it up. My story is better.

Also, once I blabbed to my folks that I saw him smoking in the movie theater, which he couldn't deny at all. I guess I'm lucky he never killed me. But in those days, it seemed like tattling was an honorable calling.

THE NEIGHBORHOOD GESTAPO

In fact, in our neighborhood especially but also throughout Dhahran privacy particularly sucked for kids. You'd have thought rules existed— How to Treat Children Ethically While Honoring Their Privacy, or some such—but no.

Parents didn't even have to live in our neighborhood to betray us; if they saw us committing some normal childhood infraction anywhere, i.e., saying a "bad word," they would immediately pick up the phone and snitch to our parents. We didn't even have to know them. And we never got to confront our accusers, which everyone knows is standard in any court of law. We were sure that couldn't possibly be fair.

I envisioned that parents had secret, likely illegal, meetings—to discuss tactics for collaboratively spying on us. Even if they didn't, the exact same effect ruled: We couldn't get away with nothin'.

Like the time Mom said I could play in the next neighborhood but only if I came home at noon. The kids there had found an awesome fort already constructed out of giant pine plywood boxes in an empty sand lot, and once we started playing "war" in it, well, time actually stood still.

Before I knew it, 1 p.m. had arrived and gone. Even if I didn't notice the time, Mom did, as did several mothers of other "soldiers." When my head popped up from a defensive turret in the fort, I spied Mom, Mrs. Williamson and some other adult spies who all just happened to be reconnoitering by in Mrs. Williamson's Kelly green, MG sports car.

Unfortunately, they saw me just as I saw them. "Go Home!" Mom yelled, and they sped off. I sprinted for home with the ridiculous idea that if I arrived first, they couldn't do anything. I would just sit on the porch, nonchalantly, as if I'd been there for ages. "What's up?" I would ask absent-mindedly.

BUSTED WHILE BOWLING

Another time, while rolling a few games at the bowling alley, according to *some* people, if I missed a spare I would lie down on the lane and roll around moaning to express the agony of my failure.

I don't remember doing anything remotely like that, of course, but a big, stogie-chomping, balding man named Mr. Brice did. And, as you might have guessed, he passed these totally spurious allegations on to my dad. I wasn't allowed to bowl again for a month. Who knew any tattletales had even been watching? But the spies, as I've explained, were everywhere.

After that trauma, I became extremely self-conscious and constricted in my bowling form (not to mention my scores), and this imposed neurosis later took over my entire personality. Today, completely due to this unjust episode, I'm an introvert.

HALLOWED HALLOWEEN

Still, everything wasn't all spies and repression in the neighborhood of 4491-B. Good times prevailed.

Take Halloween. Due to the inherent safeness of Dhahran (a result of all the spies), we kids pretty much enjoyed free range throughout town begging for treats on that sacred night. One magnet: Aramco president Mr. Davies' house, a stately 1950s contemporary on M Street—Dhahran's only two-story single-family residence—spare and clean and wide, with window walls and pale desert limestone trim. Mr. Davies' wife always gave out caramel-dipped apples I heard she made herself (not the servants, I mean).

Other than the Davies' any house on Halloween generally sufficed. When trick-or-treating, we scored a lot of Mars and PayDay candy bars, Double Bubble and blue-wrapped Black Jack chewing gum, licorice sticks, assorted packaged cookies and very occasionally a—still-warm!—chocolate brownie. Sometimes an older boy would sneak up from behind, cut a hole in the bottom of a kid's treat bag and steal whatever fell out. When we got home, Mom allowed only three treats per day from our Halloween stash. Challenging.

One unique Halloween phenomenon in Dhahran—it probably happened nowhere else in the world—involved American flyboys from the U.S. Air Base a few miles away who obtained special passes to enter the camp's residential areas that night. Wearing silky, casual, floral, Hawaiian-style vacation shirts and cotton slacks—and holding tin cups they cadged from their mess hall—they would go trick-or-treating. But instead of candy, their treat was a shot of Dhahran's ubiquitous homemade sidiqi. You'd see these guys all over town, smiling, strolling, taking in the cool autumn air, being nice to kids. Happily sipping their "sid."

'BEANIE'

One of my good friends was Bill Mandis, whom everyone called "Beanie."

Beanie had a quality I couldn't really define then but sensed: charisma. Kids seemed to naturally gravitate toward him, like moths to flame, but instead of getting burned in his presence they got stoked. A handsome kid, he also wore glasses as thick as the bases of Coke bottles, which made his eyes look twice their normal size and gave him a permanently brooding, intense effect.

Plus, he *was* intense, running everywhere at top speed, his long hair flying straight back, seemingly always with a ragamuffin gang of disciples trotting behind. I sometimes gravitated over to his neighborhood and played with him and his *homies*, but although I really wanted to be an *official* part of his group like everybody else, I mostly just visited. Memory is curious, though; recently, when Beanie and I reminisced as adults, he recalled that rather than my going to his neighborhood he always felt compelled to come to mine. Most of the "cool kids" he said lived near my house, not his. A parallel universe perhaps?

I first reconnected with Beanie in the early '80s, when we were both in our thirties. This was in Dhahran, where he had returned to work for Aramco after college. He had married a lovely woman, was a newly minted dad, and after initially working as a teacher was then a writer in Aramco's Media Department; I was working in al-Khobar as a correspondent for the English-language daily newspaper *Saudi Gazette.*

He still seemed to have the same charisma and varied talents so abundant in his youth. He had written a play after he returned to Dhahran, a comedy he also directed and local actors performed at the Dhahran theater. A witty, literate play, it impressed me. He also wrote music, which, when I heard some of it, sounded to my untrained ear comparable to that of professional musicians. His love of music apparently stemmed from his stint as a lead singer in a Dhahran teenage band.

But, still, he appeared driven, toward what I did not know. For such a charming, multi-talented man, he seemed to be trying harder than necessary to achieve … what? He was a natural, after all. He had always been a natural, in my memory.

Curiously, when Beanie and I shared childhood memories as adults, we discovered that, coincidentally, we had pursued many of the same girls in the Dhahran of our youth: Chris Reed, Janet Swindig, and Antoinette Lafrenz, to name three. Apparently, the most erogenous, primitive regions of Beanie's and my white matter—the brain stem and hippocampus—were very similarly wired. Or, perhaps, those girls were universally irresistible. Or both.

'MAD DOGS' INVADE

One day my friend Bruce Grantier and I were playing in a large, undeveloped area of town populated with mounds of sand in regularly spaced, equally sized piles, as if something would soon be built there. We climbed to the top of one pile, pounded our chests and yelled, "I'm king of the mountain!"

Off in the distance we spotted two dog-like creatures—trotting *toward* us! At that time, dogs were not allowed in camp because, we were told, they attracted "jackals," which we understood to be wolf-like but with sharper teeth and more carnivorous tendencies. Also they might carry rabies, which by itself could certainly kill you or, at least, require excruciating antidote shots in the stomach.

Neither of us had ever seen a jackal, but we could sure imagine they would look exactly like these ominous fellows fast approaching. We quickly hid in a narrow space between two dunes, not thinking that the jackals could easily sniff us out wherever we were and shred our skinny bodies in two seconds. We huddled and waited, our ears pricked up, our hearts pounding, lamenting our pathetically brief lives. Would this be the end?

Nothing happened. After a really long time we peeked out and looked around. Nada. We sprinted for home, hyper-alert, feeling like prey, jerk-looking all around like paranoid rabbits as we ran. Later that day we heard that two "jackals" had been shot by Security (Aramco "police") down by the ball field near our houses. They turned out to be just a couple of *saluki* mutts, owned by nearby Saudi camel herders, who had burrowed under Dhahran's perimeter fence looking for food.

The story improved immensely when we told it *our way*.

STREET BALL

Boyhood in Dhahran, as everywhere, involved a rich array of sports. However, kickball—basically baseball played with feet—was our main kid entertainment for years in the neighborhood of 4491-B.

Instead of hitting a little hardball with a wooden bat, kickball players kicked a big, air-filled rubber ball rolled toward them, rather than thrown. Otherwise, the two games are pretty much the same. Players run to bases in both, and score by circumnavigating all four bases, any of which in neighborhood kickball can just be a corner of a wall that you slap on the way by. A perfect natural kickball venue existed in a somewhat narrow passageway between ours and the Williamson's houses that served as our playing field. The high walls of homes on either side of the cramped area gave it the feel of a tight canyon. Yet, the walls also kept balls from inadvertently bounding away and vanishing into the void, meaning we didn't have to chase them all over creation. Perfect.

First base was the southeast corner of my family's backyard wall; second base, someone's jacket thrown on the sidewalk just west of the Congletons'; third base, the southwest corner of the Williamsons' wall; and home plate, a vague, ill-defined place just before you reached the asphalt alleyway east of our house.

Besides the ball and maybe shoes, equipment was unnecessary.

CAPTURE THE FLAG

We also played Capture the Flag in the neighborhood, especially on summer nights when the late-setting sun lit-up the world until after 9:30 (our summer bedtime graciously extended to 10).

Ours was a perfect vicinity for Capture the Flag, with lots of narrow spaces between houses to hide in, little cubby-hole concealments everywhere, and towering walls to obscure in shadow your stealthy approach to the flag.

In months when the sun set earlier, we often played in the dark, an even more intense experience, and too many of us frequently and inadvertently collided with concrete walls and each other in the darkness. More like actual combat.

'GUNS'

In fact, I spent a good deal of my childhood playing "guns"—simulated warfare—with the neighborhood gang: Beanie, Bruce, Jimmy, Steve, David, Robbie Sivak, Craig Lund, a hilarious kid named Jeff Metcalf, and a bunch of other playmates I can't remember.

When some of us (not me, of course) got cool new Daisy air rifles for Christmas, "guns" suddenly got more serious. Sometimes, a "combatant" would sneak up and—POW!—blast an air rifle into someone's ear (just air, no BBs), which still rendered the victim effectively deaf for a long while afterward.

I got a Chuck Connors *Rifleman* rifle for Christmas one year, with its distinctive round cocker. I briefly reigned as the baddest bad-ass on the block until I accidentally broke the thing later that day.

PARTIES GALORE

Besides faux combat, we also enjoyed more peaceable pursuits, such as endless Dhahran birthday parties with musical chairs, pin the tail on the donkey, piñata bashing and astonishingly complex birthday cakes, one of the happy results of having Moms with no jobs and, thus, lots of free time.

One birthday Mom and Dad together created a medieval castle cake for me, complete with defensive parapets, an army of plastic knights, turrets I could imagine Rapunzel tossing her endless hair out of, a defensive moat with blue-frosting water, and a drawbridge that actually worked. Does anyone have time to create such cakes anymore?

The "big kids" in the neighborhood had their own parties. One at 4491-B was attended by a local "Fonz"-type boy named Buzz Hall, who had swoop-back fenders *and* at flat top at the same time, as I recall. I just liked his name; for a time I considered adopting it for myself. Also, at that party some of the kids were "necking" (whatever *that* was) out in the alley, my Mom whispered with alarm, and she rushed outside to put a stop to it immediately.

Hanky-panky strained adult parties as well, Mom explained, sometimes involving neighbors who were married but not necessarily to each other. I'm told the questionable stuff usually happened in the alley, deeply shadowed by the tall walls, obscured by dense hedges and likely much encouraged by the fragrant pink-flowered oleanders and frangipani. Alcohol was also usually involved somehow.

THE (VERY) LITTLE MILLECENTO

One more story in a long chapter, this about our first and only family car in Arabia.

It was a Fiat *Millecento*, which Dad pronounced *milla-CHEN-toe*—meaning 1,100 in Italian. At the time, I thought *Millecento* meant "little" because the vehicle would have easily fit in our bathroom, small to begin with. For some obscure reason, however, my dad loved that car, which I should point out had *no air-conditioning whatsoever* in a country where summer temperatures of 115° F were, like, *average*. I remember many unforgettable one hundred-mile round trips to Little League games in other Aramco camps in the rolling boil of summer. And I don't mean unforgettable in a good way.

But sometimes, when we'd return home from a tortuous drive in the ol' *Millecento*, my dad—who had been a track star in college, a sprinter—would race me down the alley to 4491-B, a cloud of dust churned up in our wake. I *almost* won a couple of times. I might have beat him occasionally, had I not been already gravely weakened due to the *Millecento's* lack of AC.

ONE BATHROOM. ONLY.

It's worth mentioning our bathroom for its quaint *singularity*, as in we only had one.

As noted previously, all the houses in Dhahran only had one as far as I knew, certainly those of all my friends. We didn't think anything of it; normal, just the way it was. But when we returned to the U.S. in 1962, we discovered that every middle-class American home had *at least* two. Wow.

At the cusp of the new millennium, in 2000, when I returned to Dhahran with my wife, it amused me to find the community had evolved with the times. 4491-B and the other duplexes in the old neighborhood had been renovated ... to add second bathrooms.

Ah, progress.

'I USED TO LIVE HERE'

When I first returned to 4491-B about 20 years after we'd left, I rapped on its screen door off the alley late one afternoon during a quick visit to the community.

The young Aramcon then living in the duplex appeared at the door, looking cross. I said, "Hi, I used to live in this house when I was a kid and just wanted to see it again." Cooking something smoky on the stove, he seemed distracted, even annoyed by my unexpected intrusion, so I quickly withdrew.

Clearly, he had no interest in world history.

Our cozy, verdant front patio.

Towering atrium offered entry from front walkway.

Kathy, me and Helton kids in our yard.

Neighbor Barbara Williamson
dropped by for morning visit.

Beanie Mandis, the cool kid
from adjacent neighborhood.

Walkway with jasmine hedges and high walls beside 4491-B.

Parties, parties and more parties.

Mike carries a cat in our alley, with Gulf in distance behind.

West meets East in Saudi Arabia, 1940s.

CHAPTER 10
CULTURE SHOCK

NOT SURPRISINGLY, CROSS-CULTURAL curiosities inevitably emerged in Dhahran.

For example, my father developed a close friendship with a Saudi colleague—Abdul Fatah Kabli, who years later became Aramco's top executive in the Kingdom's western region, headquartered in the sprawling Red Sea city of Jeddah. The courtly and kindly Mr. Kabli had a gregarious, giggle-prone Saudi wife who often made him blush. On occasion, she purportedly nudged the boundaries of traditional Saudi decorum.

Within the rarified confines of Dhahran with its more relaxed American vibe, Saudi women could ignore some traditional protocols of behavior. Indeed, some of them daringly chose to appear in public unveiled, much to the consternation of their more conservative husbands.

My Mom told the story of how on a normal workday, Abdul Fatah walked through the aisles at the Commissary looking for a bite of lunch when he suddenly spied his *unveiled* wife pushing a cart toward him. She saw him, too. Awkward.

Resisting the impulse to do a quick about-face and flee, he kept trundling toward his wife, passing her without a glance, as if she were a total stranger. (I like to imagine she winked and giggled.) Since Saudi men outside the family had never seen Abdul Fatah's wife unveiled, no one was the wiser. She could have been *anybody's* heretofore anonymous, unveiled wife. But traditionalist Abdul Fatah knew she had tempted fate, and it embarrassed him.

REAL MEN DON'T DO IT

On another occasion, Abdul Fatah inadvertently caused *my* embarrassment.

Saudi men routinely hold hands with one another; it's normal in traditional Saudi cultural, even considered manly among closely allied male adolescents and adults. Of course, American men *emphatically* don't hand-hold, other than with very small boys.

I was eight or nine and we had just arrived back in Dhahran after a "long vacation." Every two years Aramco granted families a three-month globe-trotting excursion that allowed them to return to the U.S. for legal residency and tax purposes, and to visit relations. Upon our return Abdul Fatah met us at the airport. As we all walked across the very wide tarmac to the terminal, he immediately took my hand, something no man had ever done with me since I was, like, five. I wanted to yank my hand away and disappear into the camel grass, but American decorum and Snedeker family rules demanded I grin and bear it. The overarching imperative was not to insult this very good and honorable man, a beloved friend of my father's and our family.

The walk to the terminal seemed *at least* ten miles.

CHILD BRIDE

Another baffling inter-cultural moment involved a lively, black-haired Saudi girl my age named Fadia Basrawi, who lived in our neighborhood. Her dad personified celebrity in Dhahran as the popular announcer for Aramco TV's locally produced education shows for Saudi viewers. I never met Mr. Basrawi, but Fadia (pronounced *fa-DEE-ah*) was a regular member of our neighborhood's diverse gang of playmates.

A smart, forthright, assertive girl, Fadia seemed unusually anxious and distracted when she arrived one day at our designated playground area. "My parents have picked someone for me to marry," she revealed, obviously terrified. After all, this meant wedding a strange man who was twenty years her senior, and she was, at this time, just eleven. We American kids had absolutely no idea what to make of this strange new information. "How can a kid get married?" we wondered, and "Would that mean she couldn't play with us anymore?"

I recently emailed Fadia, who now lives in the U.S. Looking back at this distressing event in her young life, she wrote that she was furious with her father and could not fathom what had gotten into him. Her mother took Fadia's side, mostly because she thought girls should be educated before marriage—itself a radical notion for a Saudi woman in those years. Even so, her mother favored a lengthy postponement of the proposed nuptials, not outright cancellation. Fadia, however, would not budge in her opposition to a traditional, arranged match.

"I made it very clear that I would not on any condition go there, no matter what methods my father tried in getting me to agree," Fadia recalled, "The guy bowed out as he saw only serious trouble ahead, and he found some other poor Saudi girl instead."

BIRTHDAYS, SAUDI-STYLE

A birthday party that taught us a bit about Saudi traditions was one organized by the mother of Dhahran Pirates teammate Saib (pronounced *sah-EEB*) Naser.

Of course, as Americans, most of the attendees brought customary gifts, which Mrs. Naser dutifully collected and placed on a table. Later, she distributed one present to each kid, except Saib. I had no idea at the time why she did that. But I sure liked her style. I've since learned that events such as birthdays are traditionally not observed by Saudis, partly having to do with the idea that celebrating anything or anyone other than God and the prophet Muhammad is improper.

Mrs. Naser, I believe, was trying to be tolerant of American customs because she was one of few Saudis living in Dhahran camp at the time and wanted Saib to fit in with his friends. But she likely knew nothing of American birthday protocols. I assume she naturally thought it selfish and unseemly for her son to get all the gifts and his friends none and so she handed them out equitably to balance what to her might have seemed an untenable situation.

School and State

Today, Saudi children of Saudi Aramco employees no longer attend the company-funded schools, as they did in the mid-century years when I was there.

As of 1980, the government has required children of Aramco's Saudi employees studying in the Kingdom to enroll only in Saudi government-run schools. But privileged, bright Saudi students continue to study as they long have in high schools and universities in the U.S. and Europe, thus experiencing long-term and close contact with Western students.

The more cosmopolitan students thus absorb Western values by osmosis, so to speak, which makes juggling the conflicting cultural imperatives back home sometimes difficult and confusing. At the start of the new millennia in Saudi Arabia, I worked with several Western-educated Saudi women who had returned to live in the Kingdom; they reported that they were teased by more provincial extended family members and other countrymen because their Arabic was less than fluent and carried an "American accent." Particularly difficult for some cross-culturally sophisticated Saudi women is the jarring contrast of extreme modesty for women mandated by their home government and the conservative culture. In the Kingdom, the dress code is total body covering, including at least partial face veils, versus the relatively unrestricted freedom of personal appearance and behavior these women had become accustomed to living in the West.

But back in our pampered Dhahran children's world in mid-century Arabia, Saudi kids attended school with us and were just regular members of the gang. Even today, in Dhahran, with its seventy-plus non-Saudi nationalities, it's common to see cliques of kids of different nationalities walking down the street together, seemingly oblivious to their differences.

Me holding Abdul Fatah's hand.

Saudi city of Hofuf had an ancient look into twentieth century.

Future King Faisal (left) chats with royals as crown prince. (Courtesy Saudi Aramco)

Smallpox was still a danger in 1950s Mideast.

Bedouin serving coffee to Aramco employee. (Courtesy Saudi Aramco)

Young Saudis study at Aramco school. (Courtesy Saudi Aramco)

A warning in any language. (Courtesy Saudi Aramco)

For early Aramco, safety was bilingual. (Courtesy Saudi Aramco)

Saudi soldiers enter Dhahran, 1954. (Courtesy Saudi Aramco)

CHAPTER 11

DISTURBANCES
IN THE FORCE

DESPITE THE OUTWARD *Pleasantville* vibe of Saudi Arabian oil-camp life in the Age of Eisenhower, there were occasional creepy and unsettling incidents.

THE KISS

Once, when I was four or five, I remember walking down the canyon-like concrete walkway between the towering cement-block walls on either side concealing ours and our neighbors' private yards. I encountered a group of Arab gardeners resting in the shade of a high wall and they motioned for me to come over.

As I arrived at their spot, one of them roughly grabbed hold of my arm and pulled me toward him, planting a kiss on my mouth. I remember the shredding scratchiness of his whiskered face and the cracked feel of his dry lips, the alien, bone-dry scent of his breath. But mostly, I remember his and the others' laughter as I hurried away, the back of my neck burning with a shame I couldn't then process.

Years later, when I was an adult, a Saudi friend explained that Arab men, who by cultural tradition routinely kiss each other's cheeks or touch noses in greeting, don't mouth-kiss men or boys. It's considered "sexy" and, thus, always inappropriate, he said.

I *knew* something creepy was going on way back when.

TAR-BOILED CAT

Another disturbing incident occurred when I was about eight.

I was tagging along with a group of older American kids near the school complex five minutes' walk from my house. The complex presented a neat arrangement of parallel, single-story, flat-roofed classroom and admin buildings and a hulking hip-roofed, barn-like gym. Nearby a steaming, bubbling tar boiler awaited use to seal the roof of an adjacent school structure. No adults were around.

One of the kids found a cat exploring the area and casually announced that he wanted to toss it into the gleaming steel tank of boiling tar. I love cats, so the idea horrified me. Suddenly, with one kid holding the terrified, screeching, flailing cat by its neck, the group started clamoring mob-like toward the boiler. I turned and sprinted for home, never seeing the final act, but hearing hoots and hollers in the distance.

My boyhood friend Beanie Mandis told me a few years ago that he had heard of that same incident himself.

SEX CRIMES AND MISDEMEANORS, ETC.

On rare occasions, I heard about nameless, faceless, transient gardeners standing in a public alley alongside a row of duplexes, exposing their taut manhood to a horrified Aramco wife (who invariably rushed indoors).

Whatever happened to the transgressors, if anything, I have no idea. But I'm sure the transgressed harbored horrifying memories for years afterward.

Homosexual scandals were rare, apparently, but a particularly reprehensible one involved two American Aramco employees in camp who had started a local club for boys. After accusations of alleged "questionable" activities with the club's young members, the organizers were quickly and unceremoniously ushered onto an airplane and banished from the Kingdom. I didn't really understand it at the time, but I knew my parents had refused to let my brother join the club, much to his chagrin because many of his friends belonged. Dad said Aramco didn't "mess around" with such things.

I have no way of knowing whether the accusations were true. My brother remembers that a couple of years later local authorities accused an American teacher at the school of homosexuality and harboring dubious intentions toward some local boys. He likewise disappeared from the community in a heartbeat. It was the '50s, after all, an era during which the West stigmatized and criminalized homosexual behavior.

Of course, I also heard of an occasional "lovers' triangle" in Dhahran, which, as a kid, I didn't completely get. For the most part they ended spontaneously, we were told, inflicting the usual heartache and disruption on people's lives.

Dinner-table conversation at our house could be surprisingly frank and uncensored, which meant all us kids were generally aware of salacious rumors in camp, whether we understood their import or not. We learned, for example, that two married couples had affairs with each other and ended up swapping mates. They married elsewhere in new, hopefully improved configurations and returned to work for the company and live in Dhahran as revised couples.

Suffice to say, Dhahran was idyllic in its way but apparently not Edenic. Yet it wasn't really Sodom and Gomorrah, either.

UNKNOWN UNKNOWNS

Unexpected things happened all the time in the Dhahran of my boyhood, captured by the phrase "unknown unknowns" coined by former U.S. Secretary of Defense Donald Rumsfeld to explain the fog of war.

Some things we *know* we know or don't know, he pointed out, and some we don't have a clue about and have no idea we don't.

Like the time the king came to Dhahran. Why did he come? At the time, it was an unknown unknown before it happened.

King Saud ibn Abdulaziz, eldest son of the Kingdom's founder and his newly minted successor, visited the then mostly American camp with his enormous entourage not long after his father's death. Of critical relevance to this memorable event, although it was unknown to us at the time, was its covertly political nature. Two years later, the king approved use of Dhahran airfield by U.S. military forces, which in retrospect gave his earlier visit extra gravity.

In any case, I never saw the monarch himself on his first visit, but I was fascinated by the Saudi military jeeps mounted with rusty-looking machine guns that paraded around town including down our neighborhood tributary, M Street. Aramcons and their kids enthusiastically lined the street.

"The king is coming! The king is coming!" somebody yelled, but only dilapidated jeeps with mounted machine guns rolled by.

I recall that soldiers in the vehicles looked dusty and disheveled, grim-faced, like they were just returning from a dangerous, difficult desert warfare campaign. They worried me.

Skirts in Khobar, 1954. (Courtesy Saudi Aramco)

Chapter 12

SNAPSHOTS

MEMORY FADES AND degrades far quicker than man-made images. But static photographs, especially, far more than moving film, capture moments somewhat disingenuously, without the explanatory context of life in motion.

Still, much of what we remember is routinely reinforced by the ever-present still images of our lives lining walls where we live, pasted in scrapbooks or, in the modern age, stored in digital files on our digital devices and sometimes replayed in continuous reinforcing loops.

AL-KHOBAR 1954

One such image symbolically freeze-frames the essence of my boyhood in Dhahran: a black-and-white photo, circa 1954, today on the entry wall of my home.

The image depicts a normal scene on al-Khobar's dusty main shopping street, with working-class Saudis of every description and age, milling about. What I find especially captivating about the picture is the two Aramco women shown casually walking down the street, wearing *skirts*.

Western women routinely wore skirts and dresses in al-Khobar back then, and the Saudis didn't seem to mind. The Saudi women didn't enjoy the same freedom; then as now, they were required in public to fully cover their heads (if not necessarily their entire faces), as well as shroud the rest of their bodies from head to toe in silky black *abaya* (pronounced *a-BYE-a*). After the First Gulf War in 1990-1991, tolerant flexibility toward the relative immodesty of Western women vanished as the Kingdom's religious sensibilities stiffened after Iran's Islamic Revolution. Iran follows a different interpretation of Islam, Shi'ism. While Saudi Arabia is majority Sunni Islam, much of its Shi'ite minority resides in its politically sensitive eastern oil heartland adjacent to Iran across the Persian Gulf, which is officially the "Arabian" Gulf to the Saudis.

The Saudi government has long worried about potential seditious collusion between its Shiite citizens and Iranian authorities against Saudi Arabia. It's strategy to mitigate the apparent threat militantly Islamist Iran after the revolution was, in part, to become "holier than thou."

Today, although Western women in Saudi Arabia aren't officially required to veil, they are expected to publicly at least cover their bodies with the concealing abaya that all Saudi women must wear. However, inside Saudi Aramco communities including in public places, the dress codes remain more relaxed for Saudi and expatriate women, as in the mid-twentieth century.

Some Saudi women now often go unveiled and sans *abaya* in Aramco towns, and even routinely wear cutting-edge Western styles, a nod toward the practical cross-cultural realities and habits of life in such cosmopolitan communities. Once outside Aramco community gates, however, Saudi women abruptly disappear behind cloaks and veils that remain mandatory in the public.

An ongoing debate festers in the kingdom among Muslims about whether veiling is religiously or just *culturally* mandated. This is an important distinction because requirements seen as divinely ordained are rarely debatable in the Saudi context. Although some violations of traditional cultural assumptions can be nearly as passionately attacked, they are not as sacrosanct as unambiguously religious ones.

An ongoing debate festers in the Kingdom among Muslims about whether veiling is religiously or culturally mandated. This is an important distinction because requirements seen as divinely ordained are never debatable, and, although some violations of traditional cultural assumptions can be nearly as passionately attacked, they are not absolutely sacrosanct.

When we lived in Saudi Arabia in the 2000s, my wife said some of her girlfriends would shop in al-Khobar during hot months wearing the compulsory abaya—with their halter tops and short-shorts completely concealed beneath.

CAVE OF AGES

One memorable weekend day, Dad decided to photograph the low sandstone hills—called *jebels*—immediately surrounding Dhahran.

We didn't often do things just the two of us, and I was excited. Dad was quite a natural photographer and his pictures, shot with an old Kodak single-lens reflex camera, always looked interesting. He knew we would be leaving Dhahran permanently in a couple of years and wanted to have pictures of these *jebels* to take with him. For those who live in Dhahran, the tan, craggy jebels have iconic status.

I don't remember many details of that day, except what I wore (actually, what I probably "remember" is a color picture of me leaning against our black Fiat *Millicento*, looking casually disinterested). But I do well remember climbing with Dad on and around the dusty, dangerously slippery sandstone slopes, peering behind boulders, almost slip-sliding to my certain death a couple of times. Dad found some old Arabic writing on a big rock, possibly ancient graffiti, which I imagined said something like, "Ahmed is a big jerk!" But I don't know. Could have been—likely was—poetic Islamic verse.

Our discovery of a small, hidden cave that day highlighted the adventure for me. Inside we found an old, char-stained campfire made of rocks arranged in a circle. I was sure we were the first humans to view this obviously sacred, primordial site since actual cavemen sat around it in the dawn of time. Dad wasn't so taken by the "ruins," saying that it must have been recently left by homeless folks who needed a shelter for the night.

I chose to ignore his theory. In my mind, the cave represented a priceless, historical artifact, or at the very least something that I might earn extra credit for telling my teacher about.

BOWLING-PIN BOYS

I spent many a happy hour at the Dhahran Bowling Alley, often contentedly *alone*. It was a favorite sanctuary for celebrating personal freedom after my folks gave me permission to ride my bike independently anywhere in town.

The place contained twelve lanes, each assigned a "pin boy," whose legs were his only visible asset. Pin boys sat on a little perch hidden in dark shadow behind and above the pins at the far end of each lane, and between rolls, you could only vaguely see their legs hanging down, spindly because South Asians (Indians, Pakistanis) are, from what I could see of them then, among the world's skinniest people.

After bowlers knocked down pins, a pin boy would quickly descend to the floor from his half-hidden perch, retrieve the toppled pins and slot them back into a mechanical pin-holder. Then, quick-as-a-wink, he leapt back up to his perch.

I could never have recognized any of the pin boys even if I had reason to; with their faces and most of their bodies concealed in shadow, they remained forever anonymous. To some people, their anonymity seemed to make them appear disposable. For example, mean-spirited kids would sometimes purposely heave their balls down lanes when a pin boy was vulnerably exposed and distracted while replacing felled pins. Fortunately, I never saw a pin boy hit this way.

Thankfully, they were far too alert, nimble and quick. As a ball flew down the lane like a bullet, the pin boy would suddenly vanish into his lair, out of harm's way.

THE CRUNCH OF TIRES

I was inordinately fond of Dhahran taxis—mostly Chevy Impalas, as I recall—with Saudi drivers. The Aramco-subsidized taxis would take us anywhere in camp for a riyal (about thirty cents).

Riding in these sleek American-styled candy-colored sedans, festooned in colorful steering-wheel and dashboard covers dripping with Oriental carpet fringe, was always fun. I also loved the rich, gravelly crunch their tires made on the asphalt pavement—*macadam*, we called it—when they executed a quick U-turn on M Street to pick us up on our side of the road.

Particularly distinctive among automobiles that plied the community's wide, leafy streets in those days were several tiny, low-riding, three-wheeled, German-made Messerschmitt autos called "bubble cars." They looked like cockpits on wheels. It's not surprising, considering some of Germany's iconic WWII fighter planes were designed and manufactured by Messerschmitt AG, most notably the legendary Bf 109 and the Me 262, the world's first operational jet plane.

When entering a Messerschmitt car, the one-piece cockpit canopy had to be opened sideways like a music-box lid, providing access to two seats—one behind the other in a tandem arrangement. This feature likely made export easy; no need to reconfigure anything to comply with local right- or left-hand driving traditions. To me, those three-wheeled cars looked like toys with pilots zipping them around the community, and I fruitlessly longed to "fly" in one.

Adults sometimes peddled three-wheeled bicycles—grown-up versions of trikes—along camp streets. They struck me as fun, but I never got to ride any of those, either.

PARENTING ARAMCO-STYLE

Dhahran was unique, rarified by special phenomena virtually nonexistent in the States.

For example, when Dhahran parents went to the movies, they often, as they had in the States, left their kids at home with a sitter.

107

But an Aramco system was in place for at-home emergencies: A message might suddenly appear on the movie screen to the effect, "Mr. and Mrs. Snedeker, please call home." The system worked because every sitter knew to call the theater if a problem arose; whoever took the call would immediately put the message on-screen.

However, not everyone used sitters. I heard about one family in our neighborhood where the parents bedded down all their kids in a mattress-carpeted room and locked the door, so they could go the movies unencumbered. The gossip was that when they came home, to open the door they'd really have to lean into it to counteract the weight—the kids were all piled up, asleep, on the other side.

NAME DROPPING

Surprisingly, legendary American songwriter Kris Kristofferson's family lived in Dhahran from 1956-1961, including his younger brother Kraig, a blonde Tab Hunter look-alike. Kraig was a classmate of my brother's and the boyfriend of Grey LaFrenz, an all-American blonde classmate, whose dark-haired, dark-eyed sister I chased after like Charlie Brown.

Mr. Kristofferson headed Aramco's Aviation Department, which oversaw the company's airline in its heyday. Kris—his hit songs included "Me and Bobby McGee" and "For the Good Times"—never lived with his family in Dhahran although he did visit including in the summer of 1957. He had finished college and was about to begin his term as a Rhodes Scholar at England's Oxford University. After that, of course, his music career took off and he soared straight into the stardom stratosphere.

Interestingly, all the Kristofferson kids' first names started with a K, no matter if it meant the spelling would be wrong—Kris, Kraig and Karen. Kool.

THE WOMEN'S EXCHANGE

A longtime fixture in downtown Dhahran was a faux thrift-shop type place called the Women's Exchange, located in what was once Dhahran's medical clinic.

My boyhood friend Beanie Mandis reports that he and another brat, Linda Ozment (whom I didn't know well), were born in the building four days apart during its clinic iteration. (By my second return to the community as an adult, in 2000 when I was fifty, the Exchange had become a kind of upscale Goodwill or Salvation Army—mostly selling donated high-end used clothes and toys, and sometimes brand-new merchandise with tags still attached.)

Ever the punster, my dad liked to joke that husbands could take their wives to the Women's Exchange when they tired of them—and exchange them for new ones. We kids *loved* that joke. Even Mom laughed. Sometimes.

In fact, if anything was missing in 1950s and '60s Dhahran camp for a full, perfect, hilarious life, I had no clue what it might be.

Future Aramco CEO Ali Naimi (second from right) holds
baseball at Dhahran school. (Courtesy Saudi Aramco)

Dad's beloved, if cramped, Fiat 1100.

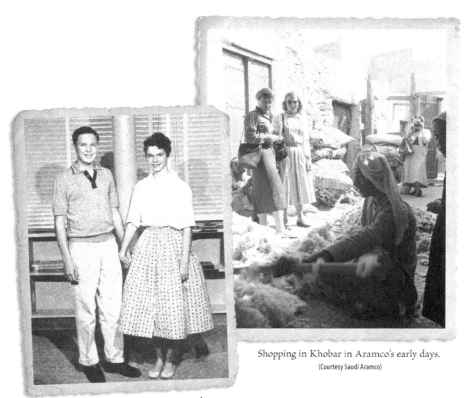

Shopping in Khobar in Aramco's early days.
(Courtesy Saudi Aramco)

Songwriter Kris Kristofferson's brother,
Kraig, with Suki Parmelee in Dhahran.

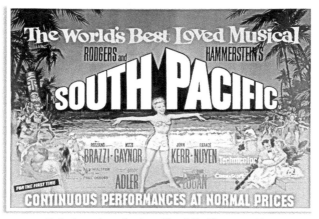

Little theater's production of South Pacific was exciting.

Pack camels lounging in al-Khobar.

CHAPTER 13

LOCAL COLOR

MY MEMORIES OF Dhahran often resemble wispy snippets of dreams, lacking linear structure or coherent narrative. Just random gauzy images, glimpses of fleeting emotion, stories with half-finished sentences despite having been retold *ad infinitum* over the dining table throughout my childhood, and unconscious embellishments slapped on as afterthoughts from my id.

Which doesn't make them any less persistent or, in my mind, worthy of passing on.

RICKETS AND 'RIVER BLINDNESS'

One of my most indelible memories is of Arabs inflicted with rickets ambling around al-Khobar in the fifties.

Some victims would have one foot pointing straight forward, the other facing backward. They looked as if they could walk equally well in either direction. The afflicted usually shuffled along with a rudimentary cane of some kind but with surprising agility.

Knowing what I do now, the past incidence of this disease in Saudi

113

Arabia seems ironic given that rickets is generally caused by a deficit of vitamin D, "the sunshine vitamin," which hinders the body's absorption of calcium and phosphorus. The condition can also afflict fetuses of women who have significant vitamin D deficits; considering the total head-and-body covering of Saudi women in the fifties, any absorption of the vitamin must have been markedly compromised. We didn't see rickets sufferers often, but when we did, we remembered.

Also, we occasionally saw an old man in al-Khobar blinded by cataracts so thick his eyes looked completely white, the pupil covered by a thick, pearly, light-blocking glaze. "River blindness," Mom said, but we had no idea what that meant because there were no rivers in Saudi Arabia, at least any places we had visited. Caused by parasitic worms carried by blackflies, the tropical disease (*Onchocerciasis*) primarily affects sub-Saharan African countries, but infections also erupt in the Americas and Middle East, particularly Yemen. It is also called "river blindness" because infected blackflies typically breed near rivers and streams.

ODDITIES

Sometimes we saw kids in al-Khobar with little stumps instead of legs, trolling along the street and down alleyways atop little wooden planks on wheels, stretching out their hands when they neared a white person. "*Baksheesh?*" ("A little money?"), they would ask.

Not uncommonly, mothers completely shrouded in black would sit on a curb, the only part of their anatomy exposed being a breast glistening in the heavy sun, feeding an infant. One idle hand would be held out absent-mindedly, hoping for *baksheesh*.

'SIGNOR FERRARI'

In al-Khobar, we frequently visited a dusty, high-ceilinged shop, where the proprietor—a guy who looked exactly like the *fez*-wearing Signor

Ferrari, played Sydney Greenstreet in *Casablanca*—always left the store's double doors and windows flung open.

Flies and dusty haze wafted lazily about. Signor Big Shop sat in a ratty, overstuffed chair in the middle of the store, like a prince fallen on hard times. The overhead fans slowly rotated, as if the electricity were weak, and the open-air feel rarely brought a fresh breeze to stir the shop's thick, aromatic atmosphere.

Signor Ferrari had a hawk that sat, glaring, on a chair arm. As I recall, the shop sold a lot of what appeared to be junk, and I remember the pale, beefy proprietor looking more Italian than Gulf Arab, his eyes nervously darting about like his raptor's.

The late author and editor (and Aramco "brat") Tim Barger, the son of former Aramco president and chairman Tom Barger, recalled far better than I do the knick-knacks sold in al-Khobar shops during his youth in Dhahran during the 1950s.

In a 2014 article in *Aramcoexpats.com* website, he wrote about another al-Khobar store particularly frequented by Aramcons in the postwar decade—the Green Flag (the Saudi flag is green). This shop, Tim wrote of one boyhood visit there, "sold stuff that absolutely no one would ever want to buy. Towels, perfume, sheets, lipstick, pots and pans, nylon stockings, sets of silverware, dishes and glasses, Waring blenders and Waterford crystal. I can't figure out how they can stay in business, but I have Pepsi on my mind." He remembered how, at the tender age of eight, he slipped alone onto an Aramco bus heading to al-Khobar, bound for the Green Flag, where he knew he could get an ice-cold bottle of Pepsi or Mirinda orange.

Barger also recalled that merchants in the Saudi town enthusiastically sold mountains of Christmas merchandise every December. Even though the shopkeepers were generally baffled by the whole concept of an endearing fat white guy in a red suit, they clearly realized that yule-crazy American Aramcons couldn't seem to buy enough of the stuff.

THE EAST-WEST STORE

Another shop, The East-West Store, also popular with Aramcons, sold glossy wood furniture from international suppliers that appeared far better quality than most al-Khobar merchandise at the time.

Many years later, after my wife and I had moved to Dhahran to work, we slipped into the store, still on the main drag, renamed King Khalid Avenue after Prince Khalid ascended briefly to the throne. We bought a Korean step-chest from an urbane, well-dressed Egyptian proprietor who managed the place.

When we went back a month or so later, the business had moved to "somewhere in Dammam," an adjacent merchant vaguely told us. But we could never find back the relocated store.

Other than word of mouth, there was no way for people to find places in al-Khobar or Dammam or anywhere in Saudi Arabia even into the 21st century. No phone books; no Yellow Pages, no convenient online directions. For me, that meant The East-West Store I remembered for 60 years had suddenly vanished without a trace.

DIY BEACHES

The gulf shore lay less than a hundred yards from al-Khobar in the mid-twentieth century. Over the years, though, dredged-up seabed reclaimed from the waterway and pile up on existing shoreline created brand new beachfront real estate, greatly broadening the shore.

Today, the al-Khobar corniche is hundreds of yards from the original downtown.

A Saudi friend told me a story about a man who bought a shoreline lot a few miles to the northeast in Dammam and built a house on it. The following year someone dredged new beach in front of him and erected a house that blocked his gulf view.

DONKEYS AND DATES

On the road to and from al-Khobar and other Saudi towns and villages in the Eastern Province, we often encountered the region's distinctive long-legged white donkeys, which were usually pulling a cart carrying a switch-flicking driver and various kinds of local commodities, like dates.

Enormous date groves carpeted parts of the region, especially around the Shiite-majority oasis town of Qatif, about an hour from Dhahran by car, which boasted rare, spring-fed canals. The delicious, light-brown dates are a traditional staple food of the nomadic *bedouin*, because the fruit is rich in sugar and nutrients; dried, it safely stores unspoiled in bedouin camel saddles during long months of annual migration over barren dessert dead zones.

Saudi Arabia remains one of the world's most prolific producers of dates.

DEAD POOL

In the 1950s, the nearby city of Dammam, situated about thirty minutes from Dhahran, presented a monochromatic uniformity, an endless jumble of light-tan mud and stucco rectangular cubes in various sizes, tightly jammed together. Everything seemed troweled with the same mud.

But, despite the cityscape's unyielding monotony, I liked accompanying my dad when he visited Dammam clients on weekends. The place was distinctly different from al-Khobar and Dhahran, quieter, and, thus, seemed exotic to me.

One Thursday morning, the first day of the Saudi weekend, Dad took me to a Saudi businessman's villa in Dammam; as we walked across a patio toward the entrance, we passed by a large swimming pool, a novelty at the time in Saudi towns. Spring had just sprung, still too cool for swimming, and the pool apparently had been ignored since the previous summer. It brimmed with gelatinous, black water polluted with floating dirt chunks and palm leaves and other microbe-slicked detritus.

The filth shocked me. After all, the Aramco pool in Dhahran always looked spotless and its water crystal clear during the swimming season, and then was tidily drained in winter. Until that moment, I thought *all* pools were like Dhahran's.

Nonetheless, when Dad and I entered the clean and elegant villa, the owner, a courtly, kindly Saudi man, directed his servant to sate me with all the delicious sweet tea I wanted. I instantly no longer cared if plague infested his pool.

THE CALL OF NATURE

Dad liked to repeat the story about the time he and Mom and another Dhahran couple drove to Ras Tanura for an evening party. Returning home later via the desolate, sandy roadway, my Mom and the other woman both had to answer nature's call, but, of course, no bathroom existed—*nothing at all*, in fact—between RT and Dhahran.

Dad, ever chivalrous, reassured them. "No problem," he said, "it's so dark no one will see you when you do your business anyway."

As the two women exited the car and squatted in the sand nearby, giggling, Dad drove off. Of course, he quickly returned, but the girls had stopped giggling by then, he recalled, grinning himself at the memory.

TORTURE TRIP

One memory remains clear for me, the boredom I felt during the last leg of the thirty-some-hour journey home to Dhahran from the States. Toward the end the flight, we flew low over the Kingdom's monotonous expanses of utter sameness, somewhat akin to *The English Patient* flying his biplane over an endless desert.

I could distinguish each individual tuft of camel grass passing by on the desert below in a seemingly endless, excruciatingly slow procession.

It took interminable, engine-droning daylight hours for us to cross the infinite desert before landing in Dhahran, and by the time we landed, I didn't care how hot or humid it was. I was *finally* home.

ALLEY FIGHTING

One day, my neighborhood gang decided when playing "War" that we needed to make things more realistic. We agreed among ourselves that if any kid really, truly got "the drop" on anyone and they were figuratively "dead men," we had to immediately fall to the ground and *play* dead.

In theory, this great, progressive innovation promised to make our faux-war seem almost real. Unfortunately, if done honestly, almost everybody "died" right away, so ninety percent of combatants immediately lay mortally wounded or completely dead on the ground, motionless, while the two or three guys still alive tried to sneak up and finish each other off. That could take twenty minutes *or more*, which seemed like forever for those of us already "dead." It's excruciatingly boring just lying there with nothing to do.

Consequently, we ended our new format and resumed the old way. Once again, nobody died because nobody would admit they'd been killed. The cynicism and lack of integrity of the combatants was still really annoying, but, then, we didn't have to wait forever for everyone to die, either.

SUN AND FLARES

Back in the day, Aramco effectively considered all the natural gas generated in tandem with the production of crude oil to be waste, even though gas is good fuel in its own right and also a feedstock for petrochemical production.

But that view gradually evolved, and by the 1980s the Saudi government decided to build a massive and massively expensive maze—the Master Gas System—to collect, process and utilize or sell the surplus gas.

However, in my youth, before gas became an environmental and economic *thing*, vertical tubes adjacent to oil wells jutted into the skyline throughout the province spewing excess gas, ignited and consumed by a constant tube-top flame—the flare—as it escaped. As we drove about at night, we saw flares twinkling across the horizon like earthly stars. Beautiful, if spectacularly wasteful, but, who knew that then?

Today, virtually all of the valuable byproduct gas is captured and processed by the Kingdom, and enormous industrial cities on both coasts utilize it mostly to create plastics such as polypropylene and petrochemicals such as the fertilizer urea, and to forge steel.

As gratuitous gas-flaring became uncool over the years, the company renamed its weekly community newspaper *The Arabian Sun*. In my youth it had been named the *Sun & Flare*.

OPENING NIGHT, SOUTH PACIFIC

Aside from the livestock-enhanced annual Nativity Pageant and Tri-District Fairs in Dhahran (more on these later), local activities involved only humans. And there were lots of such community diversions.

The local little theater group, for example, staged an abundance of shows over the years, but the one I best remember was a production of the fifties musical *South Pacific*. I especially loved the *karaoke* singability of its music. My dad, a Pacific war veteran, rocked the movie soundtrack a lot on his beloved Grundig stereo and we all belted out its songs around the house.

Dhahran's production of *South Pacific* also was exciting because I knew a lot of people in the cast, including Joe Helton, our next-door neighbor. I mean, he lived *right next door*, and there he was, up on stage... *singing!* ... in front of God and everybody. Before that, I had only seen him doing regular dad things. Other cast people I knew wore grass skirts and coconut brassieres and sang songs with bad and ungrammatical words like, "Now ain't that too *damn* bad!" from the song *Bloody Mary*.

I remember opening night like it was yesterday. The theater was packed with several hundred Aramcons, and the excitement in the air almost crackled as the local orchestra played some teaser passages—*There Is Nothing Like A Dame—Nothing. In. The. World.* Everybody in town attended, it seemed.

The event felt phenomenal, *historic*; one of the best nights of my life. A kind of "Bali Hai" moment, where you find your perfect place—"Here I am your special island. Come to me. Come to me."

DAD'S PRIDE AND JOY

On weekends, music always wafted loudly through our house. The Grundig would blast out show tunes from *The King and I*, *My Fair Lady*, *West Side Story*, *The Music Man* and, of course, *South Pacific*, and the honeyed voice of Italian tenor Mario Lanza singing arias from *Madam Butterfly* and the 78-LP album *The Great Caruso*. That stereo was Dad's pride and joy, and it provided the sound track to my childhood. Sinatra, Crosby, Doris Day, Patti Paige, Perry Como—a golden time for music, and what I still love best.

FREEDOM

For kids growing up in Dhahran, freedom set it apart.

Our parents gave us, like their plants, much more space to grow naturally than did their counterparts in the States. By the time I reached eight or nine, I had a Schwinn bike and permission to ride by myself the mile or so to the recreation complex, which included the baseball field, community library, snack bar, theater, and bowling alley. It was an intoxicating freedom, mitigated by the fact that it proved virtually impossible for a young child to get into any real trouble or danger in Dhahran without everyone immediately knowing about it.

As I noted before, adults were always keeping an eye on one another's kids. Still, I savored jumping on my trusty Schwinn one-speed, occasionally ringing its bell to draw attention, and pedaling off to the bowling alley. Once there I would roll a few games on my own, maybe watch a movie with friends, and perhaps have a chocolate shake and fries at the snack bar. We routinely tore off most of the straw's wrapper, leaving only the straw-tip covered, then dipped that into the shake and blew the chocolate-dripping wrapper bit toward the ceiling, where it usually stuck. I'm sure the Indian soda jerks didn't appreciate that, but what could we do? It was tradition.

Sometimes when school closed for a trimester break—Dhahran School operated on trimesters, not semesters, for reasons having something to do with long vacations—we kids could play almost the whole day without ever having to even talk to a grown-up. Utopia, as I said.

But because adult spies were everywhere, we had to play nice.

Desert truck groans under spheroid tank. (Courtesy Saudi Aramco)

Learning golf. (Courtesy Saudi Aramco)

Road to Ras Tanura.
(Courtesy Saudi Aramco)

Sunset prayer. (Courtesy Saudi Aramco)

Dhahran sub-sub-compact. (Courtesy Saudi Aramco)

Camel market in Hofuf. (Courtesy Saudi Aramco)

Bedouin family near Dhahran. (Courtesy Saudi Aramco)

First Aramco commercial oil well.
(Courtesy Saudi Aramco)

Camels roam Arabian dunes. (Adobe Stock)

CHAPTER 14

DESERT CREATURES

CAMEL. CAUTION!

IT'S EASIER TO thread a camel through the eye of a needle than get one to step over an oil pipeline. True fact.

Aramco in its early years went to a lot of trouble dealing with that reality.

The company transports all its oil for export and domestic use, in mid-century as now, via countless oil wells linked to processing centers and storage facilities. The arteries for this system are an endless tangle of pipelines extending countless thousands of linear miles, which Aramco in its early days patrolled by airplane looking for damage and leaks.

Unfortunately, the above-ground pipelines were loathed by famously persnickety camels; although the beasts towered up to Six-and-a-half feet tall at the shoulder, for some reason they refused to step over the conduits they easily could have. It was a camel *thing*; they just didn't like stepping over stuff.

So, Aramco had to build countless tamped-earth "bridges" over pipelines every so often along their interminable lengths, and only then were camels willing to cross a pipeline to get to the other side. Without the little manmade bridges, though, camels would keep slowly ambling alongside a pipeline … forever, if need be … or until it ended and they could walk around it. Eccentric brutes, camels.

Still, to be fair, the dromedary (one-humped) Arabian camels are miracles of nature. Native to the Arabian peninsula, the beasts are supremely hardy creatures perfectly evolved to survive in their unforgiving environment. A third, clear eyelid under the other two as well as extra-lush, double-rowed eyelashes help protect camels' eyes from blowing sand. Auto-closing nostrils keep dust and sandy grit out of their respiratory tracts.

Mother Nature has also provided these unique creatures with large, self-flattening hoof pads with rugged callouses that aid in dune walking, and the capacity to drink up to thirty gallons of water in less than fifteen minutes and then survive long periods without a single quaff. They can absorb water from their fatty humps when drinking water is unavailable, and Bedouin have reportedly coaxed camels to regurgitate water from one of their several stomachs when their handlers desperately need water themselves. Not particularly tasty, I imagine, but hydrating. Additionally, "omni-herbivore" fairly describes this no-nonsense breed, whose thick, tough lips are designed to withstand even thorny forage other desert mammals won't touch.

Camels can carry five hundred pounds of cargo, a capability that made them indispensable in trade caravans for thousands of years. Like the American bison (a.k.a. "buffalo") of the United States' Great Plains region that sustained the area's Native American tribes, camels once provided nomadic Bedouin with nearly everything to support life, including meat, milk, and leather. The iconic camels have thus long been appropriately known as the "ships of the desert." Sheep wool and mutton, plus dates, supplemented their minimalist fare.

Notoriously cranky but not particularly aggressive, when these generally plodding beasts are provoked they can turn violent. I once saw a video of a fight between two enormous male camels in which the victor gripped his nemesis' neck with his teeth, threw him to the ground and proceeded to asphyxiate his victim by lying heavily on his chest. Both camels totally ignored the vigorous and impotent protestations of their handlers.

Nomads display tremendous affection for their camels, much as American cowboys do for their horses. In fact, as an adult I attended several of what were called "Camel Beauty Contests" in eastern Saudi Arabia, where Saudi owners displayed prize beasts that sometimes fetched hundreds of thousands of dollars or more in sales. Hint: If you want to get into the business, very droopy lower lips are considered lovely and enhance a camel's value.

For what it's worth, the gravelly whine that *Star Wars'* character Chewbacca emits is a camel's groan.

Graceful gazelles

Another indigenous animal common in the deserts of the Eastern Province in Dhahran's early days was the *gazelle*, a lovely, gentle, easily tamed little antelope. Indeed, many Aramco kids in Dhahran adopted the sweet-natured creatures and kept them as backyard pets.

Young gazelles weren't much more than two or three feet tall at the shoulder and had enormous, dark, heart-melting eyes. When these slender, pale-tan antelopes ran, they presented a picture of weightless, bounding grace. Boing! Boing! Boing! But, unfortunately, they were also good to hunt and eat, and by the time we left the Kingdom in 1962, they were nearly if not fully extinct.

Sadly, as an adult I never saw a single *gazelle* in the eleven years my wife and I spent in the Kingdom after the turn of the millennium.

However, in the new millennium, wildlife conservators in the Gulf states have made good strides preserving and expanding herds of another animal: the lovely, majestic oryx, a much larger species of twin-horned antelope also indigenous to the region.

Majestic oryxes in red dunes. (Adobe Stock)

Arabian gazelles are nearly extinct. (Adobe Stock)

Arabian horses kick up dust
in a desert run. (Adobe Stock)

Salukis: desert greyhounds. (Adobe Stock)

Giant ears mark desert foxes. (Adobe Stock)

Baboons thrive in northwestern Arabia.
(Adobe Stock)

Daub lizards are ugly but durable.

White donkeys are common in Eastern Province. (Adobe Stock)

Kids playing at Dhahran School, 1950s. (Courtesy Saudi Aramco)

Chapter 15

SCHOOL DAZE

MY FIRST THOUGHT when I remember elementary school in Dhahran is always the alphabet strips above the chalkboard, white letters on a dark-green background.

For several years the strips exhibited plain block letters, but on the first day of second or third grade, I believe, I saw a magical change: the block letters had been replaced by graceful, cursive characters. They looked profound, as if suddenly I was finally on the verge of learning the secret code to all of life's inscrutable mysteries. In a way, I was.

Dhahran Senior Staff School

The Dhahran School, located near our house on 3rd Street, must have been a good school because it stimulated in me an excitement for learning and new ideas that has never dimmed.

As schools in every city and town in America, our K-9 school was a major contributor to Dhahran's nurturing communal ethos. The New York Board of Regents accredited it.

To my kid's way of thinking, the campus had everything that a great school required: a gym with a gleaming, football-field-sized (or so it seemed) hardwood floor, and magical stackable sliding bleachers—*grrrrr-CLANG!, grrrrr-CLANG!, grrrrr-CLANG!*

Each Aramco camp had its own school, administered by the company-funded education system. These schools offered traditional American-style curricula, PTAs, parent-teacher conferences, school plays, sports, and the usual din of adolescent and preadolescent angst and cluelessness.

My sister and I attended the 3rd Street School once we were old enough for kindergarten. Because my brother was already school age when we first arrived in Dhahran in 1953, he attended fourth or fifth grade at the community's then-temporary school building up by King's Road Stadium until the new school was built on 3rd Street.

Only a five-minute slow stroll from our house, the school primarily educated the children of Aramco's professional Western (then mostly American) employees. The school complex was rectangular, low-slung and '50s modern-looking with lots of windows. One-story classroom buildings predominated—two parallel and one perpendicular—which rendered the gigantic gymnasium out-of-place and alien-looking with its metal gambrel roof that evoked a Dutch barn in colonial America.

Before school, we would throw tennis balls outside against the gym's towering southern wall, standing on a broad asphalt playground that sloped sharply downward for about one hundred yards and away from the Temple of Sport.

THE 'FIGHT'

Once, during this before-school ritual, I saw classmate Ricky Hill hassling a much smaller friend of mine named Bobby Johnston, which led to my confronting him.

Immediately, we were face-to-face, scowling, but I had never even seen a fistfight much less participated in one so really had no idea what to do next. Yet, with our dukes up, we were soon circling and circling and circling each other until Miss McConkey, the playground supervisor, broke up the "fight" and hauled us into the principal's office by our ears.

Miss McConkey exuded toughness (if you messed with her, you might get "McConked," we liked to say).

Long story short, our parents were notified and the two "fighting" Rickys both got in big trouble at home that night.

BASEBALL CARDS

In general, abundant standard joys helped allay the occasional oddities of my boyhood in Dhahran. One beloved standard was baseball cards.

A lot of us boys went through a phase between eight and ten where we collected and flipped them. Each card glorified a particular professional player, pictured on the front faking some baseball motion, with his multi-year statistics displayed on the flip side—batting average, RBI's (runs batted in), triples, doubles and home runs.

We generally acquired our cards on vacations to the States (no *Amazon.com* back then), normally buying five cards in a pack of Fleer or Topps bubble gum. Mostly, fate gave us cards of guys who never hit above .220, which was lousy, and whom we had never even heard of. But if one of us happened to get a Willie Mays, Mickey Mantle or Yogi Berra card, you'd have thought we won the lottery.

Flipping cards, a preoccupation before and after school and on weekends, consisted of tossing a special "flipping card" (with meticulously curled-up corners) against a wall, hoping it would land with the player's face up. We were convinced that curling the corners made a card, spun face-up and clockwise, less likely to flip over as it twirled flatly toward and then bounced off a wall. If your card landed face-up and the other guy's down, you won whatever card your opponent bet on the flip. When I once won a Mickey Mantle off Bobbie Johnston, he cried; I lost a Whitey Ford another time to someone else and tried hard not to.

On one vacation in the States, I flipped cards with the son of my parents' friends, and he lost. He went screaming into the living room, whereupon his dad ordered him to give me his whole box of cards as punishment for being such a crybaby. My dad objected, but the other dad wouldn't have it. It was an excellent day for my collection, bulk-wise. But, unfortunately, there were only one or two decent cards in the whole bunch.

I hauled my card collection everywhere—in its annoyingly bulky shoe box—even on vacation. Usually there was no argument about it other than one time on a sunny day in Oakland, California. Mom had temporarily made Mike the boss of me for the day while she and Kathy went early to Grandma Dolly's house. Mike inexplicably refused to let me bring my enormous box of cards with me as we prepared to take a bus later to join everyone at Grandma's. What's the logic of that? He *had* to know I would never agree.

As I exited our hotel room with my arms gripping the precious box like a recovered fumble, Mike literally dragged me back in, as I kicked and yelled the whole way—"Noooooooooo!" He didn't care a bit and the cards stayed at the hotel. At grandmother's house I brilliantly presented my airtight case against such injustice, but even Grandma Dolly failed to support me (first time *ever*, I might add).

That night I was sentenced to bed right after dinner, without ice cream. Sadly, nobody understood my life's extreme difficulties at all.

Pardonez moi?

I learned many important non-academic things at school. Such as the first day of kindergarten when a polite, freckle-faced kid named Stephen Reed sat next to me during the morning snack of orange juice and graham crackers and taught me a new word.

As mannerly Stephen accidentally bumped my juice without spilling it, he said "pardon me." Pardon me? I had never heard such a thing, but it sounded important. In my house, we said, "excuse me" or simply "sorry." That's what *everybody* said. This other, more refined-sounding phrase introduced something radically new to me, a virus of self-doubt. From that day forward I started saying, "pardon me," much to the eye-rolling ridicule of my whole family.

Afternoon naptime in kindergarten was mostly entertaining, and I never napped. Algie Pechulius and I would lie on our backs, and as plump, round-faced Miss Odom walked past we'd look up her skirt and giggle.

HALLOWEEN IN DRAG

Halloween was wonderfully fun in every grade because we were allowed to wear costumes to school.

In fifth grade, my mother, in a very questionable decision, decided I should go in drag, although she wouldn't have called it that. Questionable, because Mom was the furthest thing from a gender bender you could possibly imagine. But I agreed to this and off I went, outfitted with lipstick, eye shadow, liner and mascara, a broom skirt, puffy-sleeved blouse and gypsy bandana. I've seen the pictures, and it's still embarrassing.

The next year, perhaps overcompensating, I was a pirate.

NINTH-GRADERS*!*

Of course, the exalted, final-year ninth-graders were worshipped in our school. And they actually did seem kind of divine.

In the late fifties, ninth-grade guys wore soft, pleated slacks that draped elegantly, white dress shirts with sleeves neatly rolled, penny loafers or saddle shoes and a look of languorous detachment. The girls wore sleeveless white blouses, full skirts with lots of poof, short "bobby socks" and also penny loafers or saddle shoes.

Flat-top haircuts and "crew cuts" (a.k.a. "butches") proliferated, and a few Elvis impersonators with swooped-back "fenders," long sideburns and "duck-tails" identified the rebels collectively known as "hoods." The ninth-grade girls, all quick and chirpy and tinkling like little bells, wore adorable bouncy pony tails and pulled-back, unfussy styles, along with short, perky, boyish, Italian hair-dos made popular in foreign films of the time. It is still my favorite era for American fashion—casually chic and comfortable.

We wee boys all wore striped T-shirts and P.F. Flyers "tennis shoes," with our jeans rolled up widely as though we could wear them for decades with gradual unrolling. We were hopelessly invisible to lower-grade girls; forget about the ninth-graders.

BUSTED!

I mostly did well in school, earning mostly A's and B's. But this came to a screeching halt in sixth grade, when my teacher, Mr. Dickerson, figured out what I was up to.

What happened was Mr. Dickerson gave me my first-ever D. Before, B was the worst I got.

In truth, I totally deserved it, but I had to convince my parents otherwise that this new teacher must surely be biased. In fact, the astute Mr. Dickerson had noticed something important: all my assigned essays, despite surprisingly long words and elaborate flights of literary fancy, said precisely... not much. Certainly not what the assignments required. Mr. Dickerson, a short, compactly built, balding fellow with a serious manner, figured that my sixth-grade writing was pretty much BS.

My folks marched down to the school and confronted Mr. Dickerson; he calmly showed them all my English essays that said hardly anything, and my pathetic test scores in grammar and the like. The punishment was severe: I was banned for six months from all after-school fun and, worse, TV. Instead, my parents constantly made me study (whatever *that* was).

The punishment remained in effect until I regained A's and B's. Enduring that long, brutal, agonizing punishment taught me an invaluable life lesson: bullshit, however well done, can only take you so far.

THE 'WITCH' OF 4491-B

Unfortunately, the "D" episode didn't represent my only moral failure in school. Another such transgression involved just simply going home each afternoon.

Arriving home, I would see my mother, freshly roused from her regular three o'clock nap and looking like the Wicked Witch of the East and about as cranky. Scary. So scary that one day I decided I didn't want to face her face after school. I told my fifth-grade teacher, Miss Mathews, that my mother always locked me out until five, when my dad got home from work. I hoped that by five o'clock, the deep sleep lines in Mom's face would have flattened a bit and her appearance might be less alarming.

Miss Mathews let me stay in the classroom after school that day as she graded papers but then—can you believe it?—she told Mom exactly what I said. Mom made me apologize to Miss Matthews the next day for my mendacity and slander, which felt so humiliating I cried.

The cruel irony: Although Mom looked like hell when *I* got home from school, she looked like a million bucks by the time Dad arrived.

I remember many days after school, as her sleep creases began to relax, sitting in the bathroom chatting with her as she "put her face on" for Dad, a curious ritual of mysterious cosmetic enhancements and a spritz of Chanel No. 5 perfume. Within minutes she looked like June Cleaver, the perfect mom in *Leave It to Beaver*: hair perfectly done, a crisp, freshly ironed blouse, full skirt and sometimes high heels, and exuding the clean, floral scent of perfume. All that just to cook dinner.

She must have thought Dad was really something for her to expend such energy on his behalf. I know he thought *she* was something—he constantly shot glamour photos of her and bought her jewelry and "baby doll" nighties. All very puzzling to me.

But, had Dad seen Mom right after school every day, as I did, I'm sure it would have been a totally different story.

Me (middle back) and second-grade class.

King Saud visits local schoolchildren. (Courtesy Saudi Aramco)

My mom's bad Halloween idea.

Barn-like gym dominates 3rd Street school.

American, Saudi students check out globe.
(Courtesy Saudi Aramco)

Miss McConkey, our playground czar.

Teacher Miss Crowe at Dhahran School. (Courtesy Saudi Aramco)

Intramural football at school, 1950s. (Courtesy Saudi Aramco)

A locust flies in for a landing. (Adobe Stock)

CHAPTER 16
A PLAGUE OF LOCUSTS

O N AT LEAST two occasions I remember, a gigantic calico cloud of locusts as far as the eye could see descended without warning on Dhahran, abruptly turning morning into midnight.

Years later, watching documentary films showing monster dust storms in the American Midwest during devastating droughts in the 1930s (the "Dirty Thirties"), I was struck by how similar they appeared to locust invasions that periodically descended on Dhahran. Locusts—prairie farmers call them "hoppers"—also used to commonly bedevil the American heartland.

When the giant cloud of fat insects fell on Dhahran, it would literally snuff out the sun. The sound of a billion locust wings flapping sounded like a billion decks of playing cards madly shuffling. In the enveloping darkness, people shuddered, their hysterical yelling adding anxiety to the din. The human apprehension was entirely rational: A dense swirl of locusts can strip a town of greenery in minutes.

FIGHTING BACK

I can still envision Mrs. Williamson, our neighbor, standing in lime-green shorts atop a car hood on darkened 3rd Street, helplessly flailing at the ravenous swarm with a tennis racket.

Atop another car someone else swings a baseball bat like a flyswatter. Scores of faceless people all over the neighborhood are chopping the air with blankets and sheets and towels as if they are machetes, although what such hysteria would accomplish was unclear. Of course, many people just shook their fists impotently at the sky and cursed loudly. Bad words that would fill a dictionary were screamed, most of these I had never heard at my tender age, but you know 'em when you hear 'em.

The expatriate Americans were all going completely berserk combatting this madly fluttering, biblically proportioned rain of insects. The Arab gardeners, on the other hand, seemed unperturbed, casually plucking the fat little creatures out of the air as they flew by and popping them into their mouths. I heard that they took some home for their wives to later fry in oil or boil in salty water.

The only critter more disgusting in my memories of Dhahran were the bright green, morbidly obese caterpillars that thickly populated hedges around town. For sport, we threw them against concrete walls to see who could make the biggest splat. This naturally primitive, even depraved, behavior of kids proves that mankind's hoped-for improvement is definitely a work in progress, in evolutionary terms.

But getting back to locusts, the ones that periodically enveloped Dhahran were actually of a certain species of short-horned grasshoppers in the family *Acrididae*. The name "locusts" identified them only in their destructive, swarming phase.

EYEWITNESS ACCOUNTS

A 1987 article in Aramco's in-house magazine *Aramco World* recalled the effects of the locust invasions on Saudi Arabia: "Many Saudis and expatriates in Arabia today recall seeing the sky darkened by local swarms during successive invasions in the late 1950s and early 1960s. They recall that the locusts got inside their houses; that their cars were pelted as if by hail; that they picked perching locusts off the bushes; that they photographed hoppers on the march; that their gardens were brown and bare the next day; and how a farmer in Qatif [an agricultural settlement in Saudi Arabia's Eastern Province] angrily scolded his laborers for rushing off to catch the insects [for food] instead of protecting his crops."

In 1972, long-time Kuwait resident and author Violet Dickson told *Aramco World* that locust swarms had long plagued Kuwait, a small country on the kingdom's northern border. "Clouds of them would come…" She recalled that in the early 1930s that "… as soon as you got the next shower of rain, out would come all these hundreds of young hoppers. First it was a little patch, but every day it would get bigger and bigger and hop further and further until the whole place was a seething mass of hoppers … falling into wells and into the drinking water. They came into your house; they ate the curtains, they ate everything they came upon."

But, as Dickson also explained, not everyone reacted to locusts with the repulsion of finicky expatriates. She noted that locusts were a viewed as a delicacy by Kuwaitis, as they were by Saudis: "[The children would] take off their kufiyahs—head scarves—and knock the flying ones down and catch them … When I went calling on ladies here they would always bring a tray of fat boiled locusts and take off the heads and legs and the wings and then offer them. The Bedu [desert nomads] dried them on their tents and kept them all year. The salukis [traditional Arab dogs] ate them, the donkeys ate them and the people ate them. The Bedu were really happy when they came."

Fadia Basrawi, a Saudi national elementary-school classmate who was my neighbor in Dhahran in the fifties, vividly describes a locust attack in Dhahran in her 2007 memoir, *Arabia's Hidden America*:

In a final deafening roar, a black sheet of starving locusts dropped from the sky. Running outside with banshee yells to hide our terror, we frantically waved sheets and pillow cases at the solid wall of insects descending into our front yard, with very little effect. The locusts covered every square inch of terrain, crawling and flying as they denuded every tree, bush and flower under their repulsive legs. The sky disappeared as wave after wave landed, covering everything with their stinking yellow goo. In a few minutes it was all over, the locusts taking off as suddenly as they arrived. We would all collapse in defeated exhaustion, still gripping our useless pillowcases, in a garden that had turned into a lifeless brown wasteland covered with dead locusts and beheaded flower stems, our acacia tree stark and nude with its skinned limbs, our grass no more, the ensuing silence as deafening and terrifying as the locust attack.

One morning in the early 1960s, not long after yet another full-scale locust invasion, I went outside to explore the neighborhood and saw that the sidewalks seemed alive with a curious shimmering effect. Bending down to look closer, I saw thousands of tiny beings hopping all over the place—baby grasshoppers recently hatched.

The sidewalks shimmered for a few days before going stone-faced again. I have no idea where the little guys went.

FROM WHENCE THEY CAME?

Grasshoppers in the Middle East generally live in arid environments, unnoticed, reproducing poorly and mostly keeping to themselves in relatively small numbers in their home territories when rainfall is scant, which is most of the time.

But during infrequent wet cycles, they can reproduce like a rampaging Ebola virus, sprout longer wings and dispatch catastrophic swarms thousands of feet high blanketing hundreds of square miles. Reportedly, these swarms can move several thousand miles in just a few weeks. Worse, they evolve voraciously, ravenously hungry, driven by their DNA to strip every living bush, tree or even inanimate green thing in their path. Each bug consumes its own body weight in food and fodder each day.

GOTCHA!

By the mid-sixties, Aramco entomologists, other experts and employees in collaboration with international health organizations were able to greatly reduce locust infestations in Saudi Arabia, but a few breakouts were again reported over the next few decades.

Apparently, locust swarming today can be somewhat controlled with modern scientific techniques and pesticides. To do so, though, you must *find* them, ideally, before they take off, needles in widely scattered breeding haystacks over millions of square miles in sixty-five countries. If conducive conditions suddenly align, monolithic locust clouds can simultaneously erupt in any of those countries.

Saudi Arabia is historically an especially important piece of real estate for locusts. Swarms have used its parched terrain for millennia as a breeding ground and a springboard to neighboring regions. The Bible is thick with them. Good luck trying to permanently change their karma.

Nature, as always, is persistent.

Locusts swarm in nearby Africa. (Adobe Stock)

Swarming locusts eat voraciously. (Adobe Stock)

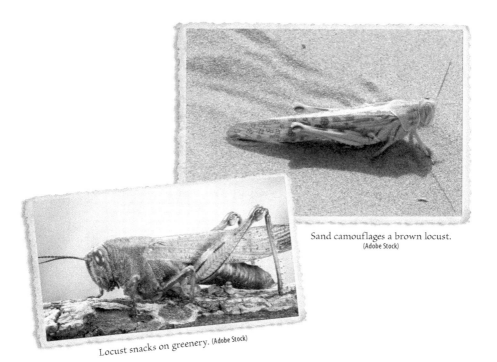

Sand camouflages a brown locust.
(Adobe Stock)

Locust snacks on greenery. (Adobe Stock)

Peeking out from dinner. (Adobe Stock)

Houseboy serves our birthday party.

CHAPTER 17
SERVITUDE

FOR MANY ARAMCONS, servants personified "the good life" in Dhahran. These ever-present helpers performed all the onerous domestic chores everyone abhors, and prepared food and served guests at Aramco communities' endless, labor-intensive parties.

Houseboys, mostly Christian and mainly from India (where St. Thomas the Apostle—apparently very successfully—introduced the faith in 52 AD), could be hired to keep your house clean, cook your meals and even raise your kids if you didn't feel like doing that yourself. The gardeners, on the other hand, were generally Arab, keeping your lawn mown, bushes trimmed and perennial plants blooming year-round. People also hired what we referred to as "ironing boys," which I don't remember much about, except ours, Mohammed, a pint-sized, soft-spoken, gentlemanly fellow from Yemen. As the job title implies, they only ironed.

FAUX RAJ

With houseboys, Americans could pretend they were actually Brits living in India during the nineteenth-century Raj, and happily rich.

151

Of course, Aramcons were none of those things. Aramco salaries in mid-century, according to my dad, were somewhat better than stateside but not exhorbitant. That made the *illusion* of wealth one of the major benefits of working for the company and living in one of its three main communities: green Dhahran; Ras Tanura, a charming shoreline place on the gulf about fifty miles away; and even barren, remote, dusty Abqaiq.

Americans in these communities enjoyed comfortable if modest-looking company housing and were charged only token rent (for U.S. tax purposes), all utilities included. This covered electricity (a gigantic perk since, if you had to pay its actual cost, electric bills would have bankrupt everybody every blazing summer). Aramcons also saved on transportation costs: Company-subsidized taxis in town were dirt cheap, which meant you didn't really need a car.

All this largess ensured that, except for the modest rent fee, day-to-day living in Dhahran was otherwise cheap or free for Western, mainly American, employees. People were at liberty to spend their salary on "whatever their little hearts desired" (as Mom often said), such as servants, fun and vacations.

The mostly middle-class Americans furnished their homes with exotic bric-a-brac that provided a nice, rich, upper-class ambience of privileged comfort: ornately hand-woven and richly colored Oriental carpets, traditional Saudi brass coffee pots, beautifully embossed copper trays from Iran, and other attractive regional artifacts.

The women had bright, fashionable clothes for every occasion, and a lot of the men even had tuxedos hanging in their closets for formal community evening events underwritten by Aramco or a night of dancing next to the community pool.

MOONSHINE

It was a lovely charade, made even giddier by the river of alcohol that flowed freely in camp (certainly in our neighborhood, anyway, and I assume ours wasn't unique).

Most of the local homemade sidiqi was distilled in complex, do-it-your-self, Rube Goldberg contraptions with mazes of copper piping jury-rigged in kitchens and special rooms in most Dhahran homes. Everyone made his or her own "hooch" at home; in fact, in its early days the company distrib-uted a pamphlet entitled "The Blue Flame," explaining how to do it safely.

As long as no one from Dhahran got hammered on moonshine and drove cars *outside* of camp at high rates of speed with half-naked, bel-lowing occupants, the Saudi government seemed to look the other way. The government was equally benign about discrete non-Muslim religious services if nobody tried to convert a Muslim to the way, the truth or the light of Christianity, or to any other creed, for that matter.

Within Aramco camps, though, this was not an issue, even though a few Saudi employees and their families resided in company communities. Christian services were inconspicuously held in the theater in Dhahran, for instance, and Muslims, if they even knew about them, would have been home with their families or at the mosque on Friday mornings, the Islamic sabbath (when weekly Christian services were also held).

So long as Christian proselytizers weren't holding public Billy Graham-style soul-saving faith-healing tent crusades targeting Saudis in al-Khobar and Dammam, the authorities didn't seem to care. Priests and pastors for American congregations in Aramco communities were discretely brought in on "teacher" visas, and none of them wore identifi-able religious dress in public, even in Aramco towns.

My dad used a small room next to the kitchen for his stash of booze and hooch-making equipment, with three-foot-tall, narrow-necked glass jars holding the sacred fermenting substances, which included some kind of grain, water and yeast. On the surface of the opaque, cruddy-looking, slowly degrading liquid floated raisins that looked to me like mouse turds, and equally questionable-looking pieces of wood—for flavoring and color, I was told. This mash quietly fermented for months in our storeroom before distillation.

To distill the end product—pure, clear, alcohol—Dad resolutely commandeered the kitchen. With the same exactitude he devoted to his color-coordinated sock drawer, he methodically crafted a marvelously efficient complex of pressure cookers, copper tubing and spouts that excruciatingly slowly drip, drip, dripped the final elixir into flasks. The distilled alcohol came out 180-proof but had to be "cut," diluted with water to a less-lethal ninety-proof to be drinkable.

This magic, high-octane stuff is what fueled the endless parties and illusory joy that informed social life in Dhahran, Ras Tanura and other Aramco towns in the 1950s. I'm not sure what other dads used to create sidiqi, but mine used raisins, yeast and grimy chunks of other stuff I couldn't quite identify. Every once in a while, someone's kitchen blew up. It wasn't usually fatal.

Aramco early on purportedly built portable alcohol stills in the machine shop that could be acquired by employees to make liquor at home. But that ended when, inevitably, an employee got arrested by Saudi authorities for moonshining. Generally, the crime was not *making* alcohol, but trying to sell it or give it to teetotalling Saudis or other Muslims. The punishment was sometimes deportation.

But, I was talking about servants.

THE GOOD LIFE

So, life was good in Dhahran at the height of the American renaissance, and well-oiled, so to speak. With a ton of *panache*. More than anything else, the luxury of having servants constantly reminded Aramcons of their suddenly elevated status—a windfall of great good fortune raining upon them from on high.

THE HELP

The servants themselves were a mixed bag. I'd like to say that they were all like British adventure novelist Rudyard Kipling's sainted Indian water-bearer *Gunga Din*, but they weren't.

As far as I can remember, most were just regular, honorable, hard-working fellows trying to support their families far from home. Their living conditions were often miserable compared to those of local Westerners, and I'm sure their salaries were criminally low by American standards. However, their paychecks were presumably tolerable or absolutely necessary for most, or I can't imagine they would have stayed.

Unfortunately, they were sometimes asked to do things that even as a boy I suspected as questionable. For instance, some wives would task a household servant with complete responsibility for their children while they played bridge or tennis or whatever all day, and then went to dinner or parties with their husbands at night.

That's the dark side of having servants. Those served tend to forget what *their* responsibilities are.

My parents were not inclined in that way. In fact, they worried so much about a little girl in Dhahran they feared was neglected and ignored by her avid bridge- and tennis-playing stepmother while being raised by servants, they briefly considered asking the parents if they might adopt her. Wisely, considering these people were friends, Mom and Dad quickly abandoned this preposterous if well-meaning idea.

Other rumors in our neighborhood insinuated that some servants' employers grievously mistreated them in some way, though details and actual evidence were always vague. The servants all seemed to me like they were doing okay, and I never saw any adults mistreat them, but some of the *kids* they minded were abusive and dismissive of their authority, and often hit them. It embarrassed me. But other kids clung tightly to their servants, and quickly turned to them to resolve disputes.

The system presented houseboys with an impossible quandary. If they ever raised a hand to a child, for any reason whatsoever—and completely justifiable reasons abounded—there was hell to pay.

MICHAEL AND LAZARUS

Early in their Aramco experience, my folks intermittently employed two Indian houseboys with unmistakably Christian names: Michael and Lazarus.

Apparently, Lazarus showed some suspect interest in my sister, and he vanished in a blink. Michael, on the other hand, proved morally unobjectionable but was as lethargic as a desert tortoise, and ill-humored. So, he received a pink slip as well.

After those guys left, we went cold turkey; the kids had to help wash the dishes—*by hand!* (dishwashers had yet to be invented)—and make our own beds. Our "Dark Age," as I think of it. But we got used to it. I can still craft a mean French corner when tucking-in bed sheets, but it brings back disturbing memories.

I'll never forget when Dad and Mom permanently decided that Dhahran's servant-rich environment might corrupt the development of their children's moral character, not to mention work ethic, an argument that at the time sounded laughably irrational to me. My friends were amused when I couldn't do something fun with them because I had to do *chores*, an embarrassing, alien concept in their minds. But the houseboy banishment proved a good thing.

Today, I even do windows, sweep things occasionally and cook a mean omelet. My character and skill set runneth over.

THE 'IRONING BOY'

My parents could not bring themselves to jettison one servant, Mohammed, our "ironing boy," because Mom really *really* hated to iron.

I remember Mom sitting on the bench seat at our kitchen's little built-in corner table, smoking Pall Malls, drinking Maxwell House coffee and chatting with Mohammed as he ironed our shirts, pants and blouses, the afternoon sun streaming in the windows. She liked and respected Mohammed.

He always came on Wednesday afternoons, punctual as sunset, arriving on his well-polished bicycle with skinny tires, a basket and a shiny steel bell. He represented immaculateness incarnate in his white-white shirt and sharply creased trousers. He was a tiny, trim, tidy man with close-cropped, almost kinky hair (like U.S. President Obama's); he had a kind, handsome face and a shy but blinding smile that always rendered me instantly optimistic.

According to my Mom, Mohammed could iron "like nobody's business," which I believed meant "really good." I don't know what they paid him, but knowing how insistently honest and fair, even generous, my folks were, I'm sure it was way above average. When we finally departed the Kingdom, Mom and Dad gave Mohammed a bonus: furniture, clothes for his family and many bagsful of other stuff, which he seemed overjoyed to get.

Just because my folks stopped employing full-time houseboys, didn't mean that they stopped using them altogether. They occasionally borrowed somebody else's houseboy for a few hours to help at a big party, but otherwise we were on our own for most of the years we lived in Dhahran. The increased need for self-reliance made us much better people than we might have turned out otherwise.

In theory.

SERVANTS REDUX

When my wife, Pat, and I returned to Dhahran to live and work in the year 2000, we were immediately set upon by aggressive Indian, Bangladeshi and Sri Lankan houseboys and gardeners desperately begging for work.

We caved, or, rather, *I* caved; Pat was sleeping at the time and said later that she'd have put the kibosh on the whole project if she'd been conscious.

All our guys proved to be kind, hard-working and fun to have around, and we paid them well above average, which appalled some of our friends. ("Good God, you're paying them *how much?*") Apparently, they believed exploitation reflected a natural and completely defensible economic tradition.

One of the gardeners, Mr. Gupta, a young Bangladeshi Muslim, wept unashamedly when we left, a generous and touching gesture of affection, and I don't think it had anything to do with his impending loss of income. He was an honorable, big-hearted young fellow, and we were inordinately fond of him, as he appeared to be of us. But, I must also admit, there is absolutely something to be said for being able to have someone else deal with those tedious, onerous, relentless chores we all loathe and neglect.

Mr. Gupta was a very competent gardener. One morning as I was leaving for work, he stopped me in the front yard to show me something in the dirt. He picked up a wriggling creature that looked like a six-inch length of fatty intestine, and, solemnly, said, "Worm." I encouraged him to murder every single one he found.

Some of us fully embraced (and without guilt) the life-soothing luxury of domestic assistance. "Don't you have a *guy* for that?" was the standard expat refrain, a backhand way of acknowledging we knew precisely how good we had it. But it kind of killed personal initiative.

As I mentioned, having servants in Saudi Arabia was not without moral hazard.

Me with one of our houseboys.

Yet another party with "help."

A look of amazement.

Mom and neighbor help out.

CHAPTER 18

DEATH IN THE AFTERNOON

T RAGEDY SEEMED SOMEHOW inappropriate in perpetually sunny Dhahran, like the sudden death of a child on a bright, carefree afternoon. Indeed, only rarely did the horsemen of private apocalypse deign to descend on our community.

But such happened one summer afternoon, a Friday after church, when a little boy playing in the camp pool with friends and family drowned unnoticed.

The cause was popcorn.

Apparently, in the teeming din of the crowded water, nobody saw the boy struggling in the shallow end and then floating, lifeless, to the surface. It seems he had been snacking on popcorn just seconds before he jumped in, my dad later explained, and some residual kernels lodged in his windpipe. The absorbent, air-puffed fluffs instantly became water-logged, and blocked the kid's airway.

Strangely in such a small town, I didn't know the boy, which made the already surreal event seem even more alien. Afterwards, whenever

I knew I would be going swimming, I refused to eat popcorn for hours before or after.

THE HANGING

Another blighted day, I awoke to a morning gloom that had settled like a black parachute over our neighborhood.

A large group of adults and kids were milling about in the alley outside our front yard, speaking furtively, as though they were afraid someone might hear. During the night, apparently, our duplex neighbor's houseboy had hanged himself in the tiny, grime-encrusted servant bathroom sandwiched between the two halves of our shared dwelling.

Nobody seemed to know why he had done it, and I had no idea how to process this news because I had never known anyone who committed suicide. I had never even heard the term, in fact, so I had no useful frame of reference. I did ponder, though, why anyone would ever decide to end his life, when existence seemed so great from my privileged, youthful vantage. Some unexplained, alien sadness, I thought. If so, how sad must someone get to arrive at such a place? Could I ever get that sad?

Since no answers were forthcoming, life went on. But in the back of my mind was a new truth: These inscrutable men who quietly tended our lives were clearly, like ourselves, vulnerable to suffering. After that incident, I never again considered servants—or anyone, for that matter—in the same cavalier, offhand way.

THE 6 A.M. PHONE CALL

Because international phone calls were so complicated to send and receive, you were almost always ready for them when the moment arrived.

But we were all completely clueless when our phone rang like a trumpet one morning while it was still dark outside, immediately waking everyone up. Sensing something dreadful, we quickly filed into the living room, where Mom was already on the phone talking to someone in a low voice. And crying.

Dick Gollan, the husband of Mom's best friend, Betty, had just called from New York to report his wife had died abruptly due to some virulent, aggressive health issue that came out of "the blue" and which the doctors couldn't fully explain.

Light didn't return to our house for days after.

I also remember an airplane crash in the gulf in which everyone aboard died, including half of a large Dhahran family, the Baumgartners (for just such a potential catastrophe, I was told, the family always split up when they traveled).

There was also another suicide in our neighborhood, but this time an expat, a mother. No explanation, as usual.

But these random tragedies seemed rare in my childhood, and afterwards life continued much as before. Contented. Undisturbed. It seemed disturbances like untimely deaths mostly happened elsewhere in the world.

It wasn't until I was in my fifties, during my third and final period in the Kingdom, that I learned Dhahran had an actual undertaker when I was a kid.

What exactly did he do all day, I wondered?

Promo for "Casablanca." (Flikr.com)

CHAPTER 19
THE SILVER SCREEN

THE CAVERNOUS THEATER in Dhahran was the incubator of my lifelong love of what were once called motion pictures. The movies.

Since evening entertainment was skimpy in Dhahran for years, especially before the company TV station debuted in 1957, my family constantly went to the movies at the Aramco theater, often three nights a week when the featured film changed.

Typically, we had dinner beforehand at the dining hall, but we still bought popcorn at the movies because Dad always wanted it; he couldn't very easily eat popcorn himself but deny us. Tickets cost the equivalent of about forty-five cents (one riyal, fifty girsh), sold by an Arab or Indian employee of Aramco. For a few girsh more, you could buy a small bag of popcorn and a glass bottle of *Bepsi* (I'll explain later) from the tiny snack bar.

People smoked cigarettes at all movie houses back then, including in Dhahran theater. A dense, smoky haze from Pall Malls, Viceroys, Chesterfields and, of course, unfiltered Camels, always wafted throughout.

We scarcely noticed; excessive smoking was normal everywhere in those days, and we were used to nothing ever looking completely clear.

BAMBI ET AL.

Sitting in that wondrous, darkened pleasure palace, we watched all the era's standard movies that had been approved for kids' viewing (more on this censorship shortly):

- Disney's animated films that became classics: *Dumbo, Lady and the Tramp, Cinderella, Bambi* (I cried when Bambi's Mom died but tried to hide it), and *Old Yeller* (I also cried when the kid had to shoot rabies-crazed *Old Yeller* but so uncontrollably I couldn't hide it).

- Adult-type films that also became classics: *The African Queen, Bridge on the River Kwai, Harvey, From Here to Eternity, Roman Holiday* (in which I fell in love with Audrey Hepburn), *On the Waterfront* (which made Marlon Brando a household name), *Oklahoma!* (in which I fell in love with Shirley Jones), *The Ten Commandments, Marty, The King & I* (in which I fell in love with Debra Kerr), *Gigi* (in which I fell in love with Leslie Caron), *On the Beach* (in which, for some unfathomable reason, I *did not* fall in love with Ava Gardner), *Please Don't Eat the Daisies* (or Doris Day), *The Alamo, The Apartment* (in which I did fall in love with Shirley MacLaine, and years later fell out of love with when she got strange), *Breakfast at Tiffany's* (in which I fell head-over-heels in love with Audrey Hepburn … again) and *Ben-Hur.*

- I also did not see the majestic *Lawrence of Arabia* until after I left the Kingdom, because it didn't come out until 1962, the year we left. But it made an enormous impression, and the grandeur and adventure it glorified was a big reason I returned to Saudi Arabia twenty years later.

I'm sure that a lot of my fundamental adult assumptions regarding morality, proper behavior, the unfathomable mysteries of women, honor and even humor are at least in part derived from the ideas I absorbed sitting in that dark theater, as the unquestioned ideals, prejudices and values of American culture flowed into me from the unfolding stories.

I doubt I'm the only one who naïvely and fully believed for a long time that *some* people are—as movies often depict them—actually perfect. The moment I suddenly realized that every single person on the planet was flawed in some way or other was on par with learning that there is no Santa Claus. And I learned that from the movies as well.

A HINT OF A KISS

"Racy" movies, as my parents called them, were off-limits for me, as were extraordinarily bloody or sadistic films, and horror pictures.

Aramco censored all films to accommodate Islamic religious and Saudi cultural sensibilities, mostly to remove scenes involving alcohol consumption or promotion and, of course, anything remotely titillating.

I can't remember if all kissing was edited out then, but it certainly was decades later when I returned to Dhahran as an adult. Actors moving in for a kiss would suddenly seem to jerk backwards, seizure-like, the curious echo of a kiss removed. Horror and violence, on the other hand, never seemed to even slightly raise a censor's eyebrow.

Yet sex remained the great boogeyman of Saudi culture into the twenty-first century.

NO SEX PLEASE, WE'RE CATHOLIC

It wasn't just prudish Saudis. Even Americans censored themselves in Dhahran.

The local Catholic priest, Fr. Roman, published movie ratings in the weekly church bulletin distributed at Mass every Friday morning. The kiss of death at the time, of course, was the "C" rating (for "Condemned"), which always pertained to movies with really fascinating characters, like prostitutes.

You went straight to hell if you watched any of those C movies, not that we kids had a prayer (so to speak) of getting in. Therefore, *Butterfield 8*, in which Elizabeth Taylor played a call girl, and *Irma la Douce*, in which an ex-cop (played by Jack Lemmon) falls for a hooker (played by Shirley MacLaine), had no chance in "h-e-double-toothpicks" (Dad's phrase) of avoiding the dreaded C rating, no matter what morally redeeming qualities the prostitutes might have.

If a film even just implied that someone was *purposely* having sex somewhere, no matter if done offscreen or between really good people, it couldn't dodge the C.

OH, THE HORROR!

As in the States, horror movies enjoyed a vogue in Dhahran in the fifties, even if banned for me.

Mom and Dad believed—correctly, I should point out—that monsters would scare the crap out of me. However, one particular horror film passed under the usually vigilant parental radar: *The Incredible Shrinking Man*. I therefore was able to watch it at the theater with a friend one hot afternoon. It may not have been a horror film per se, but it scared the bejesus out of me nonetheless.

In a nutshell, *Shrinking Man* is about a guy who drives his boat through a tiny cloud that oddly appeared on the surface of a lake where he was sailing one day. The very next day, the long sleeves of his shirt, curiously, seemed too long; the following day and the next, it grew steadily worse, until the sleeves eventually covered his fingers and then hung down limply. Unsurprisingly, this totally freaked out *Shrinking Man* and his wife. And things just got steadily worse. And worse. Until his wife had to put him in a dollhouse when she went out, to keep the cat from eating him.

Eventually, things got so bad *Shrinking Man* ended up living in a matchbox in the basement and hoisting a straight pin to defend against a giant (compared to him) black spider who lived down there. In the end, the protagonist grew tiny enough to escape by shimmying through a hole in the basement window screen. But as he scampered off through the forest-high grass, a hungry-looking bird bounded into the frame.

For several weeks after seeing that film, I fearfully looked behind the shower curtain and my bedroom door and had zero interest in seeing *Frankenstein* or *The Blob*, even if my parents *had* allowed it.

Also, I refused to have anything to do with spiders of any kind.

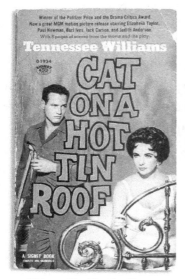

"Cat on a Hot Tiny Roof" poster.

Flyer for "Breakfast at Tiffany's."

Charlton Heston as "Moses."

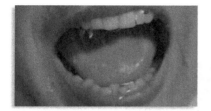

Iconic scream from Hitchcock's "Psycho."

Brando in "A Streetcar Named Desire."

"Lady and the Tramp" picture.

Sinatra in "Kings Go Forth."

Fair ride based on "Dumbo" movie. (All movie photos from flikr.com)

New Dhahran TV arrives, 1950s.

CHAPTER 20

HORSE OPERAS

A MIRACLE ARRIVES: TV

TV SHOWS WERE likely as influential as movies to the development of my adult mentality.

The wondrous technology finally arrived in Dhahran and Aramco's other camps on Sept. 17, 1957, via Channel 3, broadcasting several hours each day. By the early sixties, the station was reaching about one hundred thousand people, including some fifteen thousand residents combined in Aramco's three main camps in the Eastern Province.

A much smaller station had started broadcasting earlier, on June 17, 1957, at the nearby U.S. Air Force "Military Training Mission" at Dhahran Airport, catering to American servicemen and employees attached to the mission. U.S. airmen in light-blue shirts read the fifteen minutes of news each night at 9:45 through the Aramco system via the Air Force station. The program was broadcast to all Aramco communities in the Eastern Province. The rest of our TV came from Channel 3 in Dhahran.

Each day's Aramco Channel 3 programming began with a melodious, bass-voiced Muslim cleric chanting a passage from the *Holy Quran* in Arabic. Arabic speakers in Channel 3's broadcast area would receive the day's American-produced programs, such as *Gunsmoke* and *Perry Mason*, which were dubbed or subtitled in flawless Arabic, while the rest of us heard the original English dialogue. In the early days of Aramco TV, the English soundtracks were sometimes simulcast on FM radio.

As with movies at Aramco theaters (the only such public theaters in the country then, and until very recently), the TV programs were consciously selected *not* to offend local sensibilities, especially those related to religious and cultural taboos, often one and the same in Saudi Arabia. Popular American adventure and Old West fare met the criteria, including, for example, the punch-'em-out, shoot-'em-up cattle-drive drama *Rawhide* (which introduced Clint Eastwood as "Rowdy Yates" to the entertainment world) and the scuba-diving-hero series *Sea Hunt* (which introduced Lloyd Bridges).

Some sports, including American professional baseball, were broadcast, and a third of the programming comprised educational shows (as required by the Saudi government), such as Arabic- and English-language instruction. The schedule also included programs discussing Arabic literature, safe-driving practices, modern farming techniques and science. Aramco TV's Arabic-language service ended in 1998, when locally owned Saudi stations began broadcasting.

In the old days, all commercials promoting alcohol were blotted out by an annoying buzz coupled with a dense mesh visual overlay over the picture on the screen. This masking commenced a nanosecond after the start of a commercial. But it had an unintended subliminal effect: the image of a beer or liquor bottle you saw in only a quick glance became permanently seared into subconscious memory.

Once television arrived, one inelegant symbol of twentieth-century civilization soon began sprouting on Saudi and American rooftops throughout the province: TV antennae.

The family-friendly Saudis quickly discovered that TV was an entertainment activity the entire family could enjoy together. American Western movies formatted for TV, along with Arabic-dubbed made-for-TV Westerns—known to Saudis as *horse operas*—reportedly became a favorite genre of the indigenous population.

TV POLITICS

The Aramco station continuously walked a tightrope of consensus accommodating American and Saudi mores and values, carefully selecting programming appropriate for Saudi households in Arab towns in the province as well as Americans in Dhahran and other company camps.

Anything promoting pork, alcohol, Christianity, even some PG kissing, had to be edited out to accommodate necessities of the kingdom's prim form of Islam. Also taboo were any TV scenes in which Christian proselytizing was depicted, much less attempted conversions of Muslims to any other religion (apostasy—the turning away of a Muslim from Islam—is still technically a capital offense in the Kingdom).

Consequently, Aramco TV programs portrayed themes commonly accepted by Americans and Saudis alike, like the justice doled out in *Perry Mason*, which mirrored Saudi sensibilities on the law and order, or the universal morality of upright family shows like *The Adventures of Ozzie and Harriet* and *Father Knows Best*.

I'm a little hazy on all the shows broadcast in those years, but I seem to recall watching *The Ed Sullivan Show; What's My Line; Have Gun, Will Travel; Superman; I Love Lucy;* the "horse opera" *Wagon Train; Lassie;* the jazzy private-eye series *Peter Gunn; Howdy Doodie;* and the kid-and-his-super-dog series *The Adventures of Rin Tin Tin* and *Lassie*.

The fifties and early sixties were truly the wonder years of TV, and even though we were halfway around the world from where these classic shows were created, we still saw most of them.

A TROJAN HORSE?

While I was personally passionately devoted to TV and the movies, the new kingdom of Saudi Arabia in the 1950s was struggling to come to grips with these new technologies and entertainments. Along with a host of other modern technological entanglements and their insinuated Western values, television's powerful effects sometimes appeared to diminish local cultural and religious traditions, and often jarred Saudi sensibilities.

When Ibn Saud, the new nation's first king, wanted to introduce radio in the country in the early 1950s, the religious authorities—the *ulema*—fought it on the grounds that Islam forbade any material personifications of humanity, much less of God. But Ibn Saud won the argument reportedly by stressing, "Can anything be bad which transmits the word of God?" Religious leaders ultimately deferred but some long remained resentful.

When ibn Saud's son, then King Faisal, sought to introduce television to his country in 1964, doctrinaire Wahhabi clerics again aggressively pushed back. But Faisal prevailed. The first Saudi-produced TV broadcast in the kingdom was a recitation of the *Holy Quran* in 1965, a politically adroit choice.

Fatefully, one of the King Faisal's nephews—Prince Khalid ibn Musa'id, the son of a half-brother—was killed that August in a police shootout as he led an Islam-inspired assault on one of the new TV stations. A decade later, King Faisal was assassinated, by Prince Khalid's brother Prince Faisal; one of the theorized motives for the murder was that Prince Faisal sought revenge for Khalid's killing by government police in the 1965 TV-station attack.

In short, broadcast media have a fraught history in Saudi Arabia. But most of the Americans in mid-century Aramco communities were just happy for the wealth of entertainment options TV provided in a country with so few at the time. Most expatriates were probably only dimly aware of the underlying Saudi religious aversion to broadcast media in the kingdom that would erupt in political protest and assassination in the next decade.

Despite their American visitors' fulsome embrace of this new, magical technology, its arrival was far more subliminally unsettling and disorienting for their Saudi hosts—as an avalanche of Western ideas has been for Muslims throughout the Middle East since World War II.

Be that as it may, Aramco-provided TV and movies in my youth profoundly influenced the kind of person I became—someone with at least a capacity for wonder, I should like to think. Popular entertainment relentlessly shapes the attitudes and aptitudes of people everywhere, in ways both wonderful and tragic.

We humans are all lovers of stories. It is a glory and curse.

Aramco TV Channel 3 truck. (Courtesy Saudi Aramco)

"Leave it to Beaver" cast photo.

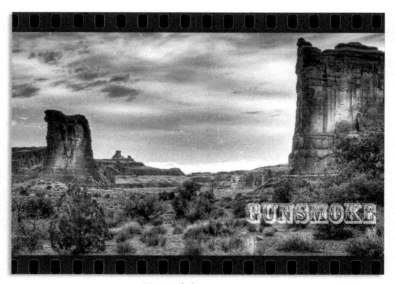

"Gunsmoke" promo poster.

"I Love Lucy" poster.

Perry and Della.

Chesterfield "tastes great."

Cast of "Lassie."

The Nelsons of "Ozzie and Harriet".
(All the non-Aramco photos are from Flikr.com)

Shinto temple steps, Japan.

CHAPTER 21
LONG VACATION

AMERICAN EMPLOYEES AND their dependents longed for "long vacation," a unique, magnificent perk of Aramco life in Saudi Arabia at that time.

Nothing compared in the States, where workaday drones were lucky to score two-weeks annual paid vacation until they neared retirement and then got maybe three. But in the Aramco benefits package at the time, all American "senior staff" employees signed two-year contracts that included: a two-week paid vacation to Europe the first year—transport and a stipend for food and lodging was included—followed by an extended "long vacation" the following year.

In our family, the short vacation was for Mom and Dad only, the long one for the whole gang. But long vacations weren't just long compared to those in the U.S. and in Europe, where virtually everyone seemed to take a month off in summer and went to the beach. No, Aramco long vacations lasted three months!

GLOBE TROTTING

On long vacations my family often flew all the way around the globe, one way or the other.

We either headed west over Europe to the States, and then, after a stateside stop, continued west over the Pacific through the Orient and South Asia on our way back to camp; or the mirror opposite, heading east from Dhahran.

It sounds kind of posh, I know, but, in fact, *everybody* in Aramco did it. Aramco paid for the round-trip air fare on long vacations, no matter which direction you went, even adding a little extra cash for "incidentals." No reason, then, not to take whatever route tripped your trigger.

I can tell you, it was not my idea that we had to wear sportscoats and neckties on those vacations, or, for Mom and Kathy, "nice dresses." In my view, such sartorial splendor made all of us look (falsely, I thought) like rich, snotty people on our vacation movies and slides, which we bored friends with later. But the reality was that this was how people traveled in those days.

If it had been up to me, my travel uniform would have been striped T-shirts, rolled-up jeans and P.F. Flyers high-tops.

But, as I mentioned, nothing was ever up to me.

SLIPPING EARTH'S BONDS

One of my favorite parts of globe-trotting was the chance to fly in beautiful, loud airplanes.

Aramco's corporate fleet shuttled mainly between Saudi Arabia and New York until the early sixties, when the company retired its in-house airline. We flew several times on what in my book is the most completely perfect airliner of all time—the TWA Constellation, a drop-dead-gorgeous, four-prop swan of a plane manufactured by Lockheed.

The Constellation's triple tail was amazing; the fuselage a slender, dolphin shape; its wings an echo of those on the macho P-38 American fighter during World War II, which sliced through the air at 375 miles an hour. Even President Dwight Eisenhower's presidential aircraft was a Constellation. Need I say more?

We once flew in the brooding, gunslinger-like De Havilland Comet, the world's first commercial jetliner, owned by Britain's state airline, BOAC (British Overseas Aircraft Corp.). A year after the plane's debut in 1952, three Comets fell apart in mid-air and dropped from the sky, which, as can well be assumed, complicated BOAC's business model. Fortunately for the company, it survived after fixing the Comet's design flaws. Luckily, we flew in the jetliner *after* the redesign.

While traveling by air, we occasionally stopped in some very strange, exotic places, including a dusty desert airstrip where we landed to refuel one humid night. The tiny, mud-walled terminal adjacent to the runway reeked of sandalwood, a rich, smoldering aroma common to al-Khobar shops. Entering the terminal, I distinctly recall a muscular falcon perched, alert but motionless, atop the seatback of a ratty rattan chair, glaring at us—with malice aforethought, I was sure.

I gave the creature a wide berth as I walked quickly past. Where was that place? I have no idea now. Timbuktu?

Years of clothes

Long vacations always involved clothes-and-footwear shopping to cover our fast-growing prepubescent bodies over the two years until the next trip.

We always patronized Capwell's Department Store in Oakland, California, and my parents bought like twenty pairs of shoes and piles of clothing in various sizes for each kid because all of us were growing like pampas grass. Nobody could accurately guess how each of our shoe sizes might grow until the next long vacation, and, if Mom and Dad guessed wrong, appropriate stopgaps certainly didn't exist in al-Khobar in the interim unless they were Arab sandals.

This meant that my folks were totally speculating on incremental sizes, hoping to bridge the growth gaps. We all walked out of Capwell's balancing tall stacks of shoe boxes along with enormous clutches of bags that contained two years' worth of shirts, pants, socks and, uh, "unmentionables," etc. People on the street actually stared, which I kind of enjoyed.

ESCALATORS! ELEVATORS!

When in New York City I was thrilled to be in department stores that featured *escalators*, which, next to airplanes, became my favorite thing.

I liked to run on them the opposite direction for which they were designed. Much to my parents' annoyance, I could be found sprinting up a down escalator and stepping down an up one. Again, not really my fault; the impulse-control synapses in my still-developing male brain had yet to link up.

Elevators held almost a similar allure. I loved riding in them in nice hotels during our globe-trotting jaunts. I was enchanted by their human operators clad in soldierly gold-and-red uniforms with shoulder epaulets, brass buttons and flat-topped caps resembling round pill boxes (like Jerry Lewis wore in *The Bellboy*). The elegant operators rotated the handles of ornately tooled brass controllers as they silently glided their elevators floor to floor, sliding open byzantine bronze gates for us to disembark.

No question: *that* was what I was going to do when I grew up.

TAILOR MADE

We once stopped in Hong Kong for a few days to be fitted for tailor-made clothes at a popular shop named Harilela's, which we kids pronounced Harry-LAY-Lees (for unapparent reasons). To us this sounded Chinese, and we incorrectly assumed that all Chinese seemed to be named "Lee" and that all Hong Kong shops were *owned* by Chinese. Neither was remotely true, we discovered later.

In fact, the Harilela's tailors and salesmen were Asian Indians, but since Indians did a lot of the work for Americans in Dhahran, I figured they were employed by the Chinese in Hong Kong as well. Turns out, the very Indian Mr. Harilela was one-hundred percent *not* Chinese, and apparently extremely rich from selling a lot of garish tailor-made madras shirts, shorts, and even, sadly, kaleidoscopic sport jackets to fad-mad Westerners.

At Harry-LAY-Lee's, all the Snedeker guys got Madras-plaid outfits, the rage then. For the next year back in Dhahran, we ran around in electric-neon, red-black-and-yellow-plaid Bermuda shorts and shirts. It's humiliating in retrospect, but at the time I thought we looked pretty sharp.

The best feature of Harry-LAY-Lee's was its *abacuses*, those ancient manual calculators, which the shop used instead of mechanical cash registers. During the endless hours we hung around getting fitted, drinking tea, me wishing I was somewhere else, one of the Indian tailors kindly taught me how to use the primeval computing device.

I thought it was genius contraption, and it gave me a new respect for antiquity.

EATING RIGHT

On long vacations, I also learned from my mother how to eat soup properly, meaning pushing the spoon *away from* instead of toward you. A little thing, perhaps, but apparently critical in polite society.

Ironically, my Mom had a lower-middle-class nature, despite her relatively up-town upbringing in Berkeley, California. Her mother, after all, was a social-climbing flapper, former debutante, five-time divorcee and a guiltless sponge off her fabulously wealthy aunt. Nonetheless, my mother decided certain particular things required decorum, including how to eat soup.

Other of her primary concerns were which knives, forks and spoons should be used and in what order (start from the outside and work your way in, she told us). And always cradle utensils gently between thumb and forefinger; never, ever clutch them in the fist as if planning to stab someone in the neck.

I'm sure learning these rules saved my reputation in society as some point, unapparent as it may seem to those who know me today.

EATING LARGE

Long vacations also were memorable for the exotic foods we encountered, such as cheese fondue, cannelloni and an intoxicating cocoa not too unlike hot liquid fudge.

I was introduced to fondue in lovely Zurich, Switzerland, when after meandering several morning hours along narrow, rolling cobblestone streets on a gray, chilly winter day, our family happened upon a little restaurant with a warm yellow interior glow. Once inside, my folks ordered the heretofore unknown *fondue*. It arrived in a large, steaming pot, placed on a rotating Lazy Susan in the center of the table; each of us got a pile of little bread chunks and a long, skinny fork with just two prongs. Oh, my goodness, that pale-yellow, Swiss-cheese fondue tasted good.

Zurich, perhaps the chocolate capital of Switzerland if not the world, also introduced me to its immortally rich hot cocoa. We luxuriated in sipping it after an elevated cable-car ride in a family-sized gondola over Lake Zurich. The gondola ride was a chance for me to subtly rock the gondola back and forth, causing it to sway, freaking out my height-averse mother. "If you don't stop doing that *this second*," she advised me (impressively, without moving her lips), "I *will* KILL *you!*" I mostly stopped.

In Rome, we once lunched at a little restaurant called The Colony, where my folks encouraged picky me to try something new: *cannelloni*. This traditional dish of tube-shaped pasta filled with meat, fish, cheese or vegetables and covered with a spicy marinara sauce looked unpalatable at first. Later, though, I had to admit it tasted *almost* as good as Chef Boyardee beefaroni.

Curiously, while I was trying to choke down this dubious tubular concoction, my Mom asked me to swap seats with her but wouldn't say why. I thought about refusing, but the odd, *yearning* look in her eyes changed my mind. Once she had displaced me in my former seat, she excitedly said to my dad, "It is, dear, it really is Buster Crabbe!" I asked, "Who's that?" and my Mom said "Tarzan, honey … But *don't* turn around."

A ridiculously handsome Olympic swimming champion like another Tarzan, Johnny Weissmuller, Crabbe had played the jungle hero in 1930s movies and later, Buck Rogers and Flash Gordon in sci-fi films. By the time Mom spotted him at The Colony, his Hollywood career was long past, but that didn't cool her excitement. I, of course, missed the whole thing, re-seated and forbidden to turn around.

Once Tarzan left the restaurant, my Mom exclaimed, "Well, *that* was thrilling!"

"You can turn around now, Ricky," she added, "if you want to."

STAR STRUCK

My parents also loved movies, which most likely is why I do, too, and they always seemed a little star-struck.

During long vacations, we went to films in Hong Kong, in English but with Chinese subtitles, or vice versa. In the sixties, I remember Dad excitedly recalling the time he waited for a cross-harbor ferry in Hong Kong with sex-symbol Chinese actress Nancy Kwan (the lead in movie *The World of Susie Wong*, 1960). Of course, 350 other people were also waiting with Miss Kwan in the ferry line. But still.

My parents' fascination with movies also partly explained why Mom got a short, chic Italian hairdo during one long vacation, in honor of Audrey Hepburn's charming Academy-Award-winning role in *Roman Holiday* (1953) opposite Gregory Peck.

CHOO-CHINE

One of my best vacation memories about Hong Kong is gangs of pint-sized shoe-shine boys that seemed to be everywhere in that city, hauling around mobile polishing kits.

"Choo-chine, choo-chine, wahn Chinee dollah!" they would pester.

Dad, ever the gentleman looking out for the underdog, always said okay and gave my brother and me each "wahn Chinee dollah." Surrounded by half a dozen Hong Kong shiners on some street corner, the three of us raised our feet one at a time onto small shine boxes, as the industrious minions polished and buffed our leather footwear to a glossy gleam while simultaneously keeping a sharp eye out for police. And then, like a random shriek in the night, they were gone.

Years later, as an adult, I surreptitiously found one of those same exact "Chinee dollahs" in a tiny shop deep in an endless *souk*, or market area, in al-Khobar, Saudi Arabia. The shop had all kinds of currencies from around the world. This lovely green bill with Queen Elizabeth's picture on it (Hong Kong was then a British protectorate) today sits on the bookshelf of my study.

It reminds me how lucky I was to see so much of our planet at such a young age. How lucky to have had parents who, with intuitive foresight, believed it would one day be valuable to their children.

GEOPOLITICS

My parents also thought it important to increase their kids' political IQ.

Once in Hong Kong we hired a driver to transport us to the Chinese border. When we arrived at the border zone, Dad pointed the one hundred yards or so to the boundary fence and darkly reported, "Over there, that's Communist China." I couldn't see anything but trees and bushes. But Dad explained that Communist soldiers were over there somewhere, *at that very moment*, watching us.

I did indeed learn something political that day: Communism. Scary.

HONG KONG

We often stopped in Hong Kong on long vacation, which made my memories of that exotic city richer than for many other places.

In the fifties, Hong Kong was a far cry from the vertical, futuristic dreamscape of glass and steel it is today; then, it was low-slung and somewhat ratty, especially the broad swaths of infested slum that clung to the hillsides. But it teemed with alien life and exotica and exuded that aromatic salt-water-and-seaweed pungency that seaside foreign ports in the Orient always seemed to have.

We always had fun in Hong Kong, going to exciting restaurants such as one on a waterfront—Aberdeen Fishing Village, it was called—where you picked the fish you wanted from a fenced pond; later the creature was delivered to your table cooked. *Voila!*

OUR SWEET AMAH

I vividly remember our Hong Kong *amah*, a female servant who minded tourists' children, including a lot of Aramcons stopping off to or from America. It wasn't that Mom and Dad were trying to ditch us; they shopped for long hours in Hong Kong and knew we would have much more fun enjoying kid-friendly activities with an amah.

I can't remember her name, but our amah was sweet and kindly dignified, taking us to parks, movies, restaurants and, my favorite, an amusement park where you could fire BB machine guns at paper targets. I felt like Audie Murphy in *To Hell and Back*.

Our amah also once took us to an engrossing park (emphasis on the "gross" part)—Tiger Balm Garden—which sported intricate, colorful murals depicting ancient scenes of gruesome torture. These included tongues being ripped out, people torn apart by horses to whom their limbs were lashed, and various other scenes of depravity. It seemed barbaric at the time, but I later learned it mirrored punishments inflicted on enemies of European rulers and on heretics by the Roman Catholic Inquisition in the Middle Ages.

Much to my parents brooding concern, I found this stuff utterly absorbing.

THE GIFT OF TRAVEL

These travel experiences would confer lifelong benefits for me, a price-less gift in my upbringing. But it didn't just happen; there was a history.

My dad's dad was a struggling newspaper editor during the Depression years, making money scarce when my father was growing up and, certainly, unavailable for foreign excursions. Consequently, when my dad was hired by Aramco and suddenly had the funds and proximity for easy travel, he grabbed the chance with gusto, as did Mom.

During the decade we were in Saudi Arabia, we traveled to England, Ireland, Hong Kong, Japan, Switzerland, Holland, Italy, and Hawaii. This exposed us largely to worlds of abundance and advantage, but seeing the hillside slums in Hong Kong, along with knowing about the widespread poverty in Saudi Arabia in the 1950s and the difficult lives of desert nomads, gave us an occasional glimpse of other, less blessed, realities the world. The so-called "other half," as my folks pointed out, was in fact how probably the other nine-tenths lived on our planet.

We kids had little understanding of how privileged and abundant our lives actually were. Even though we were not wealthy by any stretch, the opportunity-rich and uniquely gracious Aramco lifestyle sure made it seem that way.

Still, we had to admit, some of the luxuries were transcendent, such as downy hotel bedding in Amsterdam in the fifties, with its mattresses, pillows and bed coverings filled with billowy duck feathers. When we'd get to the hotel exhausted after a day's travel, we'd fall into beds so luxuriantly soft that you actually *disappeared* into the fluffy, enveloping mass. Sleep came instantly, and in the morning, you had to climb out of this deep, heavenly hole.

And the Dutch had creamy soft ice cream, too!

PARADISE FOUND

On long vacations we treasured our visits to Hawaii and the Japanese-style home of my dad's brother, Uncle Frank, his wife, Aunt Helen, and their daughters, Kela and Shelly.

Names were quirky and fluid in that family. Frank was ironically known as "Speed," because he had been such a slow hurdler in high school; Helen in middle age became "Sabrina" after adopting *Subud* (pronounced *SUE-bewd*), an obscure Indonesian spiritual practice; daughter Kela's name was lyrical and interesting in its own right, derived from a Hebrew word meaning "princess" but also a Hawaiian word meaning "one who excels"; and, finally, Shelly, who mirrored her mother's spiritual journey by embracing Subud and adopting the name "Jennifer."

Aunt Helen's (Sabrina's) backstory fascinated me: Her mother was a confederate and confidant of Margaret Sanger, the pioneering and controversial American birth-control and sex-education advocate in the first half of the twentieth century. Helen/Sabrina remained a steadfast freethinker throughout her long life, and I found her refreshingly lacking unthinking sentimentality.

As you might imagine, Hawaii is a ridiculously gorgeous place, with broad volcanic plains, breathtaking rolling hills and vertigo-inducing valleys, many-splendored flora, endless beaches of unrivaled whiteness (and sometimes blackness due to volcanic soil), and truly glorious sunsets. Even as a kid, I found the island's natural beauty staggering. And the temperature was always seventy.

One restless evening at Uncle Speed's and Aunt Helen's, I went outside into the warm rain. I ran slowly around the neighborhood for about thirty minutes, gently cooled and warmed simultaneously by the downpour, thrilled by the utter aliveness of the sensation. To this day, when I think of Hawaii, I am running in the warm rain of a Honolulu night.

I also really cottoned to Hawaii's radical casualness in the fifties and early sixties; If you wore a shirt that buttoned, you were overdressed. Girls often wore bikinis in grocery stores, and guys wore cotton shorts and those flowery Hawaiian shirts worn inside out (with the faded side out); the older women wore loose, summery, brightly floral and sometimes billowing *muumuus* (pronounced moo-moos). And the sunlight was always warm, gentle and clean.

To my mind, Uncle Speed was a life genius: Arriving in Hawaii with the Army Air Corps during WWII, he looked around and told himself, "Goodness, this is paradise. Why would anyone want to live anywhere else?" So, he lived and worked on the islands from after the war until sometime after he retired. At that point he and Sabrina moved to the U.S. mainland to be nearer their kids—first to the Seattle area and later to Portland.

Happiness, to my mind, is often just such opportunity sensibly seized.

Years later, Uncle Speed flew in to Rapid City, SD, to visit my wife and me, piloting his tiny two-seater "kit" airplane that he built himself. One day, he flew me over the site of the famous Sturgis Motorcycle Rally, twenty miles from our house.

"You fly it," he said nonchalantly, nodding toward the controls as we banked northward over the rally site. As if it were as simple as riding a bike.

I grabbed my joystick (there was one each for the pilot and passenger) and very gingerly pushed it to the right; the plane barely leaned right. "Don't be shy," he urged. So, I pushed the control stick forward more aggressively; the plane's nose suddenly dropped and we started to dive. Alarmed, I quickly pulled it back, and up came the nose again. Uncle Speed, expressionless, stared calmly out the window off to the left, as if he wasn't at all worried that death lurked in the cockpit.

Jesus, I thought to myself. *I'm actually flying this thing.*

THE GONDOLIER

A vacation highlight from Venice was the time I "helped" our gondolier row his shiny, sleek, jet-black boat through the canals.

As we passed under the watery city's countless small bridges, I felt proud under the gaze of Venetian kids peering down at us, laughing, as we floated by. I was certain they were envious. No matter; I was Christopher Columbus on the cusp of the New World.

THE EUROPA

Once in Venice during the off-season, Dad decided we should stay at a super-swanky hotel called The Hotel Europa and Britannia. Prices were low already and dirt cheap after the Italian lire's exchange against the dollar was factored in.

As always, we got two rooms—one for grown-ups, one for kids—but each was about the size of an American high-school gym, with ceilings roughly as high as the Sistine Chapel's. Due to the off-season doldrums, we were practically the only guests in the hotel, except for an old man who sat in the corner of the dining room during meals and a couple of blue-haired ladies who drank wine but seemed to never eat.

To all appearances, this enormous hotel momentarily existed just for us. In the dining room at dinner, where Dad forced us guys to wear jackets and ties, we had the undivided attention of all six waiters one night, as they stood ramrod straight. You'd take a sip of water and—zip!—one of the waiters would instantly refill your glass. Drop your fork and—zing!—a new one appeared next to your plate almost before the first one hit the ground. That night I tried veal *scaloppini* for the first time. Delicious, of course, but what I really liked about it was saying *SCAL-oh-PEE-nee* in a fake Italian accent.

"This place is only costing us thirty dollars a night," Dad kept saying. "Can you believe it?" I could because money had only abstract meaning to me as a nine-year-old. For all I knew, you could buy a TWA Constellation for thirty dollars.

DEATH IN ST. MARK'S SQUARE

About a billion pigeons resided in Venice when we were there (as I assume they still do), all pooping nonchalantly on the city's beautiful priceless architectural treasures, a chemical assault that I learned promised to eventually destroy them. I didn't care, because I *liked* pigeons.

In St. Mark's Square, where dense flocks of the winged creatures hung out, vendors sold little paper funnels full of corn kernels to sprinkle on your head, which encouraged fluttering birds to land on your noggin. When you're nine years old, what's not to like: you're suddenly the center of attention.

About 2 p.m. each day, a city employee walked around the square with two huge watering cans whose perforated nozzle caps were removed. As he walked, he poured a steady, thick stream of corn onto the ground, and, not surprisingly, what seemed like *millions* of pigeons would engulf the plaza, a swirling, flapping mass of birdkind that nearly blotted out the sun.

They also, so to speak, blotted out each other. Crushed by the rampaging mob, pigeon corpses lay scattered about the plaza when the surviving flock returned to the roof ledges after the daily feeding.

The city feeder then walked around collecting the limp victims of unrestrained nature, "red in tooth and claw," as always.

AHHH! HOME AT LAST.

Despite all the truly great experiences we had on long vacations, simply returning home to Aramco camp in Dhahran exceeded all others. Home.

The marathon of endless flights en route was brutally exhausting for a hyperactive kid like me, cooped up for eons inside cramped airplane fuselages. When I finally got home, ragged with fatigue and jangled brain chemistry, I often felt hopelessly depressed, requiring a good twelve hours of solid sleep to recover my good humor and sunny optimism.

The first night back, as I lay in bed waiting, yearning for sleep, I always felt doomed, an evil sinner deserving of perdition, the grim reaper waiting expectantly just outside my door, scythe in hand. And then consciousness blessedly departed.

By the next day, the dark cloud started to lift as I headed outside to find and play with my friends in the glare and blister of the Saudi sun. All was well again in my mind in our little American utopia.

Winter pit stop, Ireland.

Aramco airliner's engine.
(Courtesy Saudi Aramco)

Dad's "junk" photo, Hong Kong.

Kids at "Red" China border.

Feeding the pigeons, Venice.

Kathy at emperor's palace, Japan.

"Wahn Chinee dollah."

With Grandma Dolly, Hong Kong.

Boarding *The Flying Camel.* (Courtesy Saudi Aramco)

CHAPTER 22

A PLANE OF OUR OWN

IN 1957, MOM and us kids were assigned an entire Aramco airliner to ourselves. The occasion for this great good fortune was a special medical visit to the States.

My brother Mike needed to go to San Francisco to be fitted for a hearing aid and learn lip-reading (and I was scheduled to receive lip-reading instruction as well because I had started exhibiting signs of encroaching hearing loss). It turned out we were both the unfortunate "beneficiaries" of a congenital sensory-neural defect in our middle-ear cochleae.

My brother was young enough at the time, about fifteen, that company policy required that a parent accompany him on any such a medical trip to the States, which created a dilemma. Aramco policy prohibited employees' children from staying in camp without their mothers, which precluded Mom and Mike traveling to America alone because then Kathy and I would have been left in Dhahran without our mother. Dad couldn't go due to work responsibilities. Therefore, the only option was for Mom to take *all* us kids to the States.

Bottom line: the *whole* plane was ours to fly to America, along with a complementary stewardess.

Once we lifted off, the Flying Camel's four engines roaring their approval, we practically had the run of the aircraft. Informality ruled in the cabin. The stewardess worked in her stocking feet, and we were allowed to race up and down the aisles. Sometimes the pilots even let us hang out for a few minutes in the cockpit, where they showed us their dials and gizmos and throttles. Best of all, in the back of the plane were *sleeper berths*, like in Pullman trains, with crisp sheets and puffy pillows, and windows to watch the slowly brightening pink clouds at sunrise.

Despite the fun, the interminable flights were draining; playing a few thousand hands of Crazy 8's with my sister en route proved deeply disorienting. By the time we arrived in New York, I was suffering nightmares populated not only by crazily animated 8s, but homicidal 6s, fiendish 4s and terrifying manifestations of every other number.

Still, I survived, and we soon transferred to a commercial airliner in New York for the onward flight to California. Eventually we registered at the Lake Merritt Hotel in Oakland, near my Grandma Dolly's home in the lovely little bedroom community of Lafayette.

READING LIPS

On weekdays, my brother and I took a bus into San Francisco to a speech-and-hearing clinic, where we were taught lip-reading. For my final exam a few weeks later, my instructor took me to San Francisco's posh Mark Hopkins Hotel, where he bought me a gigantic root beer float and asked me to tell him what the people were saying at a table across the room. "We ... maybe ... be ... go ... bunny," I told him. I blew into my straw once, for no particular reason, and in some sort of chemical reaction, root beer foam instantly exploded out of my glass and covered much of the table. Fortunately, I wasn't graded.

GRANDMA'S HOUSE

Grandma Dolly's two-bedroom home was a charming, low-slung, fifties-style ranch on Birdhaven Court, lined with other similarly clean and tidy houses dripping with Weeping Willows in their front yards.

People who had been classmates of my parents in high school in Lafayette still lived on the street, which seemed odd; surely, they would have moved away by then, I thought, assuming that all Americans were as mobile as my family.

Grandmother's yard was rain-forest lush, and she employed a Japanese gardener who wore one of those pith-helmet type deals with mesh draped over his face, like a bee-keeper. He worked busily, never talking or even acknowledging anyone, so I figured he didn't know English and that he might be a recent immigrant. As a kid I had no awareness that generations of Japanese had been American citizens long before the war. Quite possibly, Grandmother's gardener was one hundred percent American and had never even been to Japan.

A towering canopy of curved, converging trees like opposing parentheses graced the narrow, hushed lane behind Grandmother's house, creating the effect of a natural-maple cathedral nave. Looking back, it reminds me of the naturalistic nave in Spanish architect Antoni Gaudí's surreal basilica in Barcelona.

I loved walking down that cool, shade-muted path of asphalt behind Grandma's house to the nearby elementary school, where I often shot hoops alone. It was my kind of religious experience.

PAROCHIAL SCHOOL

During another visit to California that was more extended than usual during a long vacation, we kids were temporarily inserted into an Oakland Catholic parochial school for six weeks to be sure we wouldn't lose too much knowledge while away from Arabia.

The teachers were stern-faced nuns who rapped our knuckles with wooden rulers for various arbitrary infractions impossible to avoid or even comprehend. Once, for chewing gum, a nun made me to stand in a corner with my nose pressed against my wad, which another nun had forced me to stick on the wall. I thusly felt the full force of the love of the Lord, who, one should think, wouldn't sweat such small stuff if he were truly *the* Lord.

Mostly, life at that school is a blur, though I vividly recall taking a lunch pail to school decorated with cartoon characters and containing a little thermos jug. In Dhahran, we walked the three minutes home for lunch, so lunch-bucketing was a new experience for us. Excitement enhanced the opening of our colorful lunchboxes on the playground each school day to discover what treats Mom had placed inside. Wonder bread and bologna sandwiches smothered in mayonnaise were a favorite, because we didn't then have bologna in camp or that fluffy, tasty, nutrient-free American balloon bread.

But, aside from opening maybe a lunch box or two, I don't believe I had any religious experiences at that parochial school. But I caught a glimpse of hell.

Saudi sweet tea. (Flikr.com)

CHAPTER 23
SWEET TEA

WHEN EXPATRIATES DESCRIBE their experiences to the less traveled, it often starts with food.

In Saudi Arabia, because the traditional cuisine is so minimalist—spare, unpretentious fare derived mainly from ancient nomadic bedouin culinary habits—only two items come quickly to mind: *kabsah* and sweet tea.

Kabsah is a mild but delicious melding of white rice; mutton, lamb or camel meat (and sometimes chicken); pine nuts; and golden, raisin-like sultanas. It is the cultural go-to entrée in Saudi Arabia.

'LAMB GRAB'

In the fifties and sixties, and even today, when Westerners attend traditional Saudi gatherings where a meal is offered—known affectionately by expats as a "lamb grab" or "goat grab"—kabsah is often served. It arrives on a large platter to be placed on the ground, and sometimes its tender camel calf lies on bed of rice.

At a "lamb grab," all attendees eat with their hands, which requires particular skill, especially when eating rice. This is the process: You squeeze some of the sticky stuff in the rough tube created within the curled fingers of your fist; then, using the thumb, you quickly slide the rice "tube" upward into your mouth. In theory. Usually, when expats do it, more rice ends up back on the platter than in the mouth.

Eating the meat is obviously easier: Grab a hunk off the carcass, insert, chew. Traditionally, the host or closest Saudi will pull off select pieces of the most tender, flavorful part of the cooked animal and hand them to the guest. This is a charming and very tasty, if less-than-hygienic, custom.

COFFEE ARABIC

After the main feasting, slightly bitter, cardamom-laced Arabic coffee is served in tiny, handle-less cups holding about a cupped-palm's worth of liquid.

Bedouin traditionally grind the roasted beans with a mortar and pestle and then brew the grounds in boiling water over a campfire. In summer, with throats hot and parched, nothing in the world cuts the dust better, in my opinion. Culturally, drinking more or fewer than three cups of this unusual-tasting coffee is considered less than polite; to signal that you are finished, you hold your cup out and gently rotate it back and forth between your thumb and forefingers when the server approaches. Coffee is also often served before dinner.

SUGAR WITH A LITTLE TEA

Sweet tea—and by "sweet" I mean, like, pure-sugar sweet—is also offered before and after meals, and at random other times as well.

With what I know now, I suspect it's lethal to diabetics. But as a kid, I experienced it as completely benign, liquid candy. Still do. And I *have* diabetes.

'PLOW'

Another rice dish we enjoyed in the Kingdom, this one of Indian origin, is *pilau* (which we pronounced "plow"). Our Indian houseboys—when we had any—prepared it.

Although *pilau* can contain meat, I only remember eating the meat-less version as a side-dish. Ingredients included *basmati* rice, cumin seeds, onion, cardamom pods, cloves, turmeric, bay leaves and cinnamon. Warm and delicious. The Lazy Boy of comfort foods in our house.

SHAWARMAH

I don't remember them as a kid in Dhahran (though I'm sure they were available), but when I first returned to the Kingdom as an adult in the early eighties a local cuisine staple favored by Western expats was *shawarmah* (roughly pronounced *shah-WAR-ma*) sandwiches.

To prepare shawarmah, succulent roasted lamb or chicken shaved from a vertical meat rotisserie, like Greek *gyros*, are wrapped in pita bread with a mild, tangy white sauce, pickles, red onions, spices and sometimes French fries. They have the exact same effect as Lay's potato chips: you can never eat just one.

As an adult living in al-Khobar, I frequented a Lebanese café just downstairs from my apartment overlooking Dhahran Street. An enormous, sweaty, joke-cracking Lebanese guy named Ahmed (aren't they all?) manned his shawarmah rotisserie on the sidewalk outside. In the evening's relative cool, he created luscious made-to-order sandwiches for three riyals (about eighty cents), selling them to whoever walked by.

An excellent night for me was buying three of these delights dripping with white sauce and slowly consuming them upstairs while watching TV and unwinding from the day's assaults.

PEP FLAKES

As a kid in Dhahran, for breakfast I favored Kellogg's Pep Flakes, a whole-wheat cold cereal that was originally introduced in 1923.

A smiling guy in a red baseball cap graced the box. Of course, Pep Flakes, which tasted a bit like Wheaties, called for milk with lots and lots of sugar, but what really mattered were the "free" little plastic army figures inside each box. Some of the diminutive, green soldiers were poised to throw a grenade, some reclining and ready to fire an M-14 carbine or a machine-gun, and many others affecting martial poses I can't remember.

When my friends and I collected a decent-size army of these little Pep Flakes guys, we would set them up on either side of a fake little "river" we created with a garden hose, and then "bomb" them with large rocks until all you could see were tiny plastic arms and legs sticking out from under the rocks and mud. I *loved* Pep flakes.

POWDERED WHOLE MILK

Real milk, though, which Pep Flakes required, didn't exist in Dhahran in the fifties. At least not straight from the cow; no mid-century dairies operated in the kingdom.

So, we had *powdered* whole milk, from Australia I believe, to which we just added water, and—ta-DAH!—real milk. My old friend Beanie Mandis recalls the brand name, Starlac—"And it seemed to go sour overnight in our fridge," he said.

When my dad brought a then newfangled Waring milkshake mixer to Dhahran—the first ever in our neighborhood—the *true* value of the powdered whole milk became obvious.

Dad used to hold milkshake "court" at our house on Thursday afternoons, whipping up shakes in his beloved blender. He made them for me and my friends who showed up, meaning *all* of them, and sometimes kids I didn't even know very well. That's the power of milkshakes.

Dad did the exact same joke every week: When he finished the first batch of pale, miraculous shake, pouring it extra slowly from the shiny metal mixing tumbler into a tall glass, he would ask of no one in particular, "So, you wanna biiiiiiite?" meaning a bite of milkshake (whatever that meant). After a lot of furious little-kid head nodding, Dad would take one kid's arm, open his mouth really wide to show his big sharp teeth and then lunge like he might actually bite it. Shrieks all around.

He made it up to the boy, now cowering and giggling, by giving him the first glorious glass of milkshake, usually chocolate. I am obsessed with chocolate milkshakes *to this day*.

'BEPSI'

Arabia also provided other tasty things to drink, such as *Bepsi* Cola—with a B—not Pepsi, because the P sound doesn't exist in the Arabic language. So, all the Saudis said Bepsi, which meant the Americans did too, by default.

Of course, even mispronounced it tasted exactly the same as actual Pepsi but proved far more entertaining to say: "I'll have a *Bebsi* and some potato *chibs*, please."

Similarly, Pizza Hut has franchises in Saudi Arabia today, but if you read the Arabic part of the logo, it says *Bizza* Hut. Back in the old days, Bebsi—"the light refreshment" was its corporate catch-phrase—was the only soft drink around. (I read that Coca-Cola and the Saudi government were at odds in the early days, so Coke products weren't distributed in-Kingdom.)

Nonetheless, downing an ice-cold Bebsi was a satisfactory substitute on a broiling hot day, of which there were literally thousands. Today, inexplicably, I'm a Coke man.

I guess being restricted to Bepsi in my youth must have had more imbact than I thought.

BANANA WORMS

Bananas were problematic in Dhahran. We never ate a banana before peeling the skin back and bisecting the fruit lengthwise.

To look for worms.

Call it a paranoid ritual, if you want, but not infrequently we found a fat, black, sometimes hairy, caterpillar-like creature nestled in the banana's central groove. You did *not* want to eat one of those things, or anything it had touched. Wormy bananas went straight into the garbage.

THE DINING HALL

Never questionable, however, was food in the cavernous, high-ceilinged Dhahran Dining Hall, which served as the town's buffet-style primary restaurant and chief meeting place.

It's tall exterior walls were blocked with pale white, irregularly shaped limestone from the Dhahran area that was also used on a number of other eminent structures in the community. Gulf limestone provided a distinctive signature building material for our town. In the early days, Italian stone masons were specifically hired to create what became the community's iconic limestone structures. These buildings give Dhahran an enduring colonial look.

What made the Dining Hall great was the well-lighted ambience provided by its giant floor-to-ceiling windows, its towering ceilings (they seemed one hundred feet tall to me as a kid) and the bracing *whiteness* of the interior. It looked as swept of germs as a hospital operating room.

Also, we had family traditions associated with the Dining Hall, my favorite being breakfast after Friday mass—eggs over easy, mounds of crispy, aromatic bacon, steaming hash browns, and waffles. Mm-MM!

I loved to watch the Indian cooks in their aggressively Cloroxed uniforms behind the horseshoe-shaped buffet line. Scores of tiny, gleaming ceramic bowls were perfectly aligned in rows on the counter beside the cooks, each containing two cracked eggs, which were slid as needed onto a broad matte-steel cooking surface, the whites crackling and bubbling in the sudden, searing heat. Snap, pop, spit, sizzle. Not to mention the piles of bacon and waffles to accompany them. For me, breakfast rules.

BREAKFAST BY DAD

On Thursday mornings, the first day of the Saudi weekend, Dad cooked breakfast for us at home.

As meticulous a chef as he was a sock-drawer organizer, everything he cooked tasted wonderful—without the same magnificent surroundings as the Dining Hall, perhaps, but great in their own way just the same.

His fried eggs were perfect, with no ragged contours on their outer edges, or undercooked jelly-like areas in the middle, and his pancakes were equally flawless. Sometimes, he would separate egg yolks and whites, beat the whites to the consistency and color of whipped cream and fold the fluffy poof into pancake batter. The resulting cakes were light, airy and the thickness of a metro phone book.

He also had a lust for bacon, which I *totally* got. It's genetic, I'm sure.

Mom's 'California Casserole'

For her part, my Mom prepared an array of modest but tasty dishes that I will long remember.

One interesting invention of hers were mouth-watering, butter-saturated, mashed-potato balls rolled in crumbled Kellogg's Corn Flakes and then baked. They were the size of softballs. I've never seen anything like Mom's potato balls since, so I like to think they're unique in the world. She also baked hugely addictive chocolate and banana cream pies, with light, flakey, lardy crusts, and fillings with a consistency that was at the exact perfect midpoint between firm and loose.

I also must mention what she called her "famous" California Casserole, with ingredients I once assumed were derived from California's top culinary delights. But the recipe seemed to change with each batch, sometimes radically, leading me to wonder. Today, I would guess that the real name should have been: All The Stuff That's On The Verge Of Going Bad In The Fridge And A Couple Other Things I Threw In For The Heck Of It Casserole.

On occasion, the concoction proved spectacularly tasty, but it was always a unique culinary adventure.

THE DEEP-FAT FRYER INCIDENT

Also burnished in my long-term memory is the deep-fat fryer my folks brought back to Dhahran from the States.

If memory serves, they fried only fresh shrimp in it, and home-made corn chips for quasi-Mexican food they sizzled-up about once a decade. Unfortunately, one day my Mom dropped the boiling, brimming, grease-slicked thing on the floor, burning herself *and* a houseboy (who, naturally, was only on hand for some temporary function). Neither victim was seriously scalded, but a chaos of yelling and general hysteria ensued for a few minutes after the mishap. Shortly thereafter, the fryer abruptly disappeared into the mist of banished Snedeker family history.

Thankfully, however, at least the pastel-green milkshake mixer proved immortal. It *still* lives on in one of my siblings' garages, I'm pretty sure, like a long-lost ancient Greek manuscript in a medieval monastery vault.

DOWN UNDER ICE CREAM

Ice cream was flown in from Australia and ended up in the Commissary; it came in giant tan cardboard tubs that probably held five gallons, and we stored them in a chest freezer at home that smoked like dry ice.

Just as Ford automobiles once came in any color you wanted as long as it was black, this Australian ice cream came in any flavor you liked as long as it was vanilla. At least no other flavor ever graced *our* freezer. No matter. That Australian ice cream elevated deliciousness to a new level of delectability, distinguished by the delicate zest of freezer-burned cardboard I grew to appreciate.

Eat your hearts out, Ben and Jerry.

Kabsah with rice, mutton. (Flikr.com)

Delicious *shawarmah* sandwiches. (Adobe Stock)

Dhahran powdered whole milk. (Flikr.com)

Just like Dad's Waring blender. (Flikr.com)

Pep Flakes
(soldier inside!).

Pepsi in Arabic is "Bepsi."

Dhaharan Dining Hall.

Fiesta Room burger and shake. (Flikr.com)

A picture of grace. (Courtesy Saudi Aramco)

Chapter 24

PUPPY LOVE

AT AGE FIVE, in Dhahran, I discovered girls. It might as well have been gravity.

One day, I suddenly noticed that girls, previously drifting about completely under my radar, were utterly alluring. I could sense it was transformational, a kind of *"BOING!"* moment.

However, because my libido was still a work in progress and largely subconscious, I mostly found the whole epiphany puzzling. What the...?

Nonetheless, when the first tiny light in a young boy's erotic pleasure center blinks on, it's not to be denied. Thereafter, this mysterious, heretofore hidden place, technically identified as the brain's lateral orbitofrontal cortex, would begin ruling my existence. Like Napoleon Bonaparte.

The little brown-haired girl

Roughly about this time, a siren-song of a girl named Pamela York flipped my main switch. In my memory, she had enormous dark eyes, full lips, long light-brown hair and a soft, round sensuality, although I knew no words that long or stimulating at five.

Our relationship played out playfully, as all kindergarten relationships do, though she did once agree to show me hers if I showed her mine. We were inseparable for … weeks. Cuddling inside a giant, open-topped block box, glancing furtively into each other's eyes, forgoing recess altogether. Sacrificing recess!? It must have been true love. Kindly, chubby Miss Odom, our teacher, oddly seemed not to notice.

THE REED TWINS

In later grades, the reedy Reed twins, Kay and Chris, captured my fancy.

They were trim, compact tomboys with inviting, toothy smiles, and they were adopted, which seemed really exotic at the time. Where did they come from, I wondered? Ireland, it turned out.

Kay and Chris both entranced me exactly the same and not just because they were identical; both had a sprinting, lust-for-life charm as little girls. But perhaps their most potent allure derived from their almost absolute disinterest in me as a male object of affection. Not that that ever dissuaded me from relentlessly trying to attract their attention.

Never happened.

In sixth grade, with my family set to return to the U.S. "for good," as we used to say, Mrs. Reed kindly organized a going-away party for me and invited all my friends, including her daughters. I received a giant bon-voyage card that everyone signed saying how much they'd miss me, and I kept it for years. But I left Arabia, still unnoticed by the Reed twins, and memory slowly receded.

Years later my sister orchestrated a brief reunion between Chris Reed and me at Arizona State University—we both had serendipitously enrolled at the same time—and I realized not much had changed between us over the years. She was still cute; I was apparently still not magnetic.

Seeing her again was lovely; she obviously had remained plucky and spontaneous, full of life. Still bathed in the poignant glow of my youth.

GROUPIES

And, of course, I mustn't forget to mention my *groupies,* if that's the right word, considering I've always had zero musical aptitude.

They were enormously sweet and, for reasons I still cannot fathom, seemed to find me irresistible at age six. We would sit together in the library, and they—one a comely blonde, the other a rather round and freckled redhead—would pass me love notes across the table. Seriously.

At first it embarrassed me, but soon I felt a little like a celebrity and just couldn't bring myself to *not* bathe in the glow of their adoration. It quickly became a little tedious, however, because there are only so many ways you can write, "You are *so* nice!!"

THE EQUESTRIENNE

In mentioning horses and girls, I can't forget Janet Swindig, an award-winning equestrienne classmate in maybe fourth grade.

Shorter and more compact than the lithe Reed twins, she, unlike them, also seemed to actually appreciate me. We played a lot of ball-bouncing foursquare during one trimester break from school, and her strong, fluid movements captivated me as she darted about. Watching her more than the ball, I remember losing a lot.

Despite my crush on her, we were just pals, simply having fun hanging out together and playing games. That kind of easy, platonic camaraderie with the fairer sex proved far more evasive as I grew older.

I remember pictures of her on the wall at the Hobby Farm snack bar, leaning hard into a sharp turn during a barrel race, gripping her horse's reins tightly. Beautiful.

And there were others:

Red: I briefly chased after fiery, flaxen-haired Janice Cyr, a dynamo with a *look* in her eye and an aggressive certainty that kind of unnerved me. In her presence, I always had the sensation that my hair might catch fire at any moment.

'Frida': Another enchantress was Antoinette LaFrenz, whose coal-black eyes, dark hair and intense, brooding eyebrows, I realized much later, were identical to those of Frida Kahlo, a striking Mexican avant-garde artist who died in 1954. Our relationship was all about roller skating in the patio adjacent to the Bowling Alley. Her sister, Grey—as blonde as Antoinette was not—looked like the actress Grace Kelly.

The goddess: Another little girl, Linda Handschin, a sixth-grade class-mate, I just admired from afar (across the room). She was the most gorgeous being of any species I had ever seen by the age of eleven, even in the movies—long, glossy black hair to her waist, a Botticelli face, a slender, fragile-looking frame. I'm not kidding; she was *something*. Smart as a whip, Linda was also a perfectionist, once dissolving into tears when she got *only* a B+.

The bikini: I would be remiss if I didn't recall the enchanting girl who fluttered the hearts of every eight-year-old boy (and probably guys of any age) in Dhahran in the mid-1950s and who also, coincidentally, made camp history. Let's call her Candy Maybe. Think of her as a brunette Sandra Dee with attitude. One summer late in the decade she returned to Dhahran from high school in Europe and—this is the historic part—wore an itty bitty black bikini to the pool as though it were allowed. I mean, whole countries banned the things in those days.

No joke; Dhahran was never the same after that.

The beatnik: I can't forget Madelle Bowman, another exotic Dhahran teen beauty with a name so perfect you couldn't make it up if you wanted to. She was my brother Mike's girlfriend, or at least I'm sure that must have been his plan. Totally understandable; she was Audrey Hepburn with curves and cool, and a jet-black pony tail with a large knot on the end like an Olympic hammer-throw. For some strange reason, she was really nice to me.

The proposition: I recall one disquieting incident involving a beautiful, mysterious neighbor girl. As I was innocently playing with her one day—we were about eight—she invited me into her bedroom. Her dad was at work; her mother was who knows where. There, in the morning shadows cast through the half-closed Venetian blinds, she changed into a silky summer dress in a closet. When she emerged, she asked if I wanted to see what was under her skirt. I looked but it was too dark to see anything, and I went home a bit unnerved. Later, though, I wondered if I might get to try again. But it turned out to be strictly a one-time deal.

Regarding the fairer sex, as time wore on I generally followed the advice in 1 Corinthians 13:11, "When I was a child, I spoke and thought and reasoned as a child. But when I grew up I put away childish things."

Except, of course, when it came to the sirens of my youth, who exist still in my memory but, like Plato's *Forms* of perfection, I assume also exist in the entire male collective unconscious forever.

Eternal, like Aphrodite.

Mary Barger, president's daughter.

Siren on horseback. (Courtesy Saudi Aramco)

One of the equestrian Flehartys. (Courtesy Saudi Aramco)

Young girl at Hobby Farm.

Farida Sowayigh.

Mike's classmate Annie Bryan.

Camille McCann, also
his classmate.

Star equestrienne Janet Swindig. (Courtesy Saudi Aramco)

Cheering on her Dhahran team.

Me on a bored donkey at the fair.

CHAPTER 25

THE TRI-D FAIR

EVERY COUPLE OF years Dhahran hosted a Tri-District Fair—the Tri-D.

It was a big deal.

The "districts" comprised the three main Aramco camps—Dhahran, Ras Tanura ("Cape Oven," in Arabic), and Abqaiq ("Father of Sand Flies")—located about an hour or so from one another. Camp residents flocked in huge numbers to enjoy these bi-annual springtime gatherings, even though it could still get miserably hot. In fact, one year my Mom fainted from heat stroke, dropping like an anvil on King's Road Stadium's outfield grass.

My most vivid memory of the fair is wandering around one morning with my friend Algie Pechulis, waiting for the action to begin. In an incredible happenstance, we happened upon a male donkey emptying his bladder, the most astonishing sight *ever*—like a fire hydrant uncorked. Algie and I stood slack-jawed at the truly awesome power of nature. The statue-still, slowly blinking donkey, though, seemed to have zero comprehension of the rare potency he possessed.

TURTLE RACES

The turtle races were always a hoot.

The little buggers "raced" on a raised, round, moat-encircled platform about fifteen feet across, with a hundred or more Army-green turtles with white numbers painted on their backs corralled under a wire-mesh dome in the middle. I'm told the turtles were procured from freshwater wells in the spring-fed, date-palm oasis of Hofuf a few miles away.

Anyone who wanted, including kids, could place two-riyal (about sixty-cent) bets on which numbered turtle would ambulate fastest to the moat and tumble in. When the dome rose, a loud chorus of deafening turtle encouragement began, followed by pitiful moans when particular favorites just froze, still as a stone—as turtles are wont to do.

I won a lot of money at those races. The equivalent of $1.80 once. But mostly I liked how everybody went insane when the basket rose and the turtles—well, a few of them—started scrambling for the moat. It created the loudest noise I ever heard.

Beanie Mandis tells of arriving at the turtle tent the final day as the Fair was wrapping up. "One of the grownups said, 'Hey, kid, want a turtle?'" he recalls. "I went home carrying twenty-eight numbered turtles in a cardboard box."

DONKEY RACES

The Fair's ever-popular donkey races also drew big crowds.

Algie's and my new best friend "Ahmed the Fire Hydrant" no doubt participated. If he ran as hard as he peed, no rider could have possibly stayed on him.

During these races, we laughed until our sides hurt as adults we knew frantically tried to stay atop bored donkeys trotting half-heartedly around a track. The problem: the "jockeys" rode bareback, so there was nothing to hang on to but the donkeys themselves. By the end of the race, contestants still mounted usually had their arms wrapped desperately around their steed's neck, their feet either dragging on the ground or one leg swung desperately over the beast's back for a couple of seconds before the hapless rider slid off. Sometimes, the winner fell off his donkey at the finish line, slamming into the ground with an explosion of dust. As an older kid, I raced one year. Came in third, still sort of mounted.

For the smaller kids, apathetic midget donkeys the size of Grand Canyon burros provided slow rides around a little circular track enclosed on either side by stick fences woven with dried marsh reeds. When you're five, it's exciting.

CAMEL RIDES

The Fair's beloved camel rides provided a herky-jerky experience something like riding rodeo bulls drowsy on Prozac (slow motion and no spinning).

When camels stand from a kneeling position, their butts jerk up first, followed by their torsos, which, if you're sitting on the hump saddle feels like you're first going be ejected forward over the camel's head, and then a couple of seconds later like you're going to get catapulted backwards over his hump. All the while, the creature is expelling rumbling, homicidal noises. UmmmNggg! UMMMNGAANG! Once the beast is up and walking, it feels as if you're on an unstable rocking chair, liable at any second to being flung what looks like two hundred feet to the ground.

Nearby Saudi *bedouin*, indigenous desert nomads, and area farmers and ranchers provided the Fair animals. They delivered their livestock to the large grass field adjacent to King's Road Stadium and watched over the critters during the event.

Food booths offered diversion, too, but I can't picture the delicacies, although I'm sure they included hamburgers, hot dogs, French fries and ubiquitous ice-cold Bebsi.

OH, THE HUMANITY!

Thousands of adults and kids crowded the fairs, a throbbing, surging mass of humanity.

All those people in one place at one time personified the immensity of the Aramco venture in Saudi Arabia in the middle of the twentieth century, an undertaking that would have such momentous positive consequences for the Kingdom, America, and the world. But, day to day, snug in our little camps, in our close-knit neighborhoods, our lives seemed comfortable, normal, in no way momentous.

Some years after we left Dhahran, Aramco abruptly discontinued the Tri-District Fair. Unverified theories abound about the reason. But I don't care. What matters to me is that I was there then, when it was glorious.

Fair crowds were huge.

Food, talk big part of fair fun.

Not exactly the Kentucky Derby. (Courtesy Saudi Aramco)

Even kids bet at turtle "races." (Courtesy Saudi Aramco)

Scout competes in bean race. (Courtesy Saudi Aramco)

What's a fair without watermelon?
(Courtesy Saudi Aramco)

Silly memento photos.
(Courtesy Saudi Aramco)

The donkey races were co-ed. (Courtesy Saudi Aramco)

King's Road Stadium, 1955. (Courtesy Saudi Aramco)

CHAPTER 26

FIELD OF DREAMS

I PLAYED LITTLE LEAGUE baseball in mid-century Saudi Arabia with the gusto of legendary Green Bay Packers head coach Vince Lombardi, who once infamously proclaimed, "Winning isn't everything. It's the *only* thing."

For me, *baseball* was the only thing.

Playing the beautiful game gave me self-confidence. Over and over again, it taught me, a decent athlete but not a star, that maximum effort and tenacity—plus pure luck—often trumped exceptional talent.

THE 'SWEET SPOT'

One of the joys of baseball is its physicality—pure movement infused with mystical grace.

For instance, one can spend years in childhood learning to hit a baseball yet only achieve mediocrity. However, if you're persistent, a seemingly miraculous, defining moment sometimes occurs: One day, with a casual swing, I unexpectedly hit a baseball so squarely in the bat's "sweet spot" that my hands felt only a soft, pleasing thump as the ball rocketed far into the outfield. "Oh," I mused, "*that's* what the coaches were talking about." Just "meet" the ball, they always said, "and it'll go." When it happens, it's transcendent.

But hitting is only part of it. Like all little boys who love baseball, I wanted to be a pitcher. The gravitational center of attention on the field, pitchers radiate glamour. I wanted that attention and validation, that specialness. But, sadly, I was a worse than mediocre pitching prospect, so early on I chose to be a catcher. If, I couldn't be glamorous, I'd at least be busy: catchers fundamentally participate in every play, every pitch, and always have something to do, if only tossing the ball back to the pitcher. Unlike outfielders, who often endure long barren stretches of inactivity, marooned in the distant outfield grass, reduced to picking their noses, kicking absent-mindedly at the turf or watching airplanes fly over.

Luckily, one of our coaches, Bev Boston, had once been a catcher in the professional big leagues in the States. He taught me a lot, such as always keeping my arm cocked and ready to throw whenever I had the ball. "It'll save you an extra second when the time comes to throw," he said, "and that can be a lot." Which turned out to be true.

JOY

I never achieved greatness as a catcher or hitter in Little League (or thereafter) but was better than many in in the fields of dreams I frequented and loved—and because I had earned my modest status with diligent effort, I often felt entitled to relax and enjoy it.

I loved playing the game and gradually if slowly getting better. It defined my childhood in many ways and provided much of its happiness and sense of future promise.

In part, the joy derived from Aramco's beneficence. I doubt many towns our size in the mid-century U.S. had such a Little League field of dreams to play in. King's Road Stadium offered generous bleachers on both the first- and third-base lines; an always freshly painted two-story announcer's booth (in which my Dad sometimes served as the announcer); a pampered topsoil infield that Aramco workers watered, raked and rolled to level perfection; a luxurious outfield lawn kept green and trimmed with constant manicuring; and bright, white chalk lines from home plate to the outfield fence marking the field's first- and third-base boundaries.

SAUDI SOUTHPAW

Although the Arabian American Little League actually had few Arab players, my team, the Pirates, had one Saudi kid on the roster—our centerfielder, Saib Nazer. Saib was an intractably non-ambidextrous southpaw, meaning his right hand was effectively useless. He thus caught *and* threw left-handed. Unfortunately for Saib, because baseball-mitt manufacturers catered to the majority righties, they produced few right-handed gloves. This meant Said had to remove his glove to throw every time he caught a ball. Which he did with surprising fluidity.

After each contest, both ball teams retired to a shady, hedge-encircled patio just beyond the outfield and next to the movie theater, where we inhaled soda pop and those wonderful little square, White Castle-like hamburgers that had the gummy texture of food prepared much earlier. All of this was provided by Aramco and served by white-uniformed Aramco food service employees, most of them Indians.

Reflecting the town's cross-cultural vibe, the green scoreboard just beyond the fence at right-center field displayed innings and scoring in both Arabic and English numerals.

NATIONAL PASTIME

Because it was the *Mad Men* era and baseball very much remained America's national pastime, and also due to limited camp entertainment options, the bleachers were often packed for Thursday morning and afternoon Little League games.

The contests were between Dhahran's Pirates (my team) and Steelers (Beanie Mandis' team), or with visiting Aramco teams from Ras Tanura and Abqaiq. Our Pirate uniforms were boring green and dishwater white, and the Steelers' were navy and Clorox, but the RT Falcons' colors were vivid purple and orange, which I totally envied. The hapless Abqaiq Cardinals, perpetually in the league cellar because remote Abqaiq (pronounced *AB-cake*) had the smallest camp with the fewest kids but the most eye-popping uniforms. Their colors of candy-apple red and snow-blind white seemed impossibly bright against their rocky, dingy desert ball field.

Despite their magnificent uniforms, the Cardinals almost always lost.

THE NATURAL

One year, however, the Cardinals had a special kid, Dennis Graham.

Even at ten, he looked like a coach, which, considering he was also a flame-throwing fastball pitcher, intimidated the heck out of us soft-cheeked boys. But one fine day, I got three hits off the guy in Abqaiq, including a triple, despite being nearly blinded by the aggressive white-ness of his uniform. A fluke, obviously.

I can clearly picture the tall, platinum-haired Graham pitching a subsequent game in Dhahran, this time against the Steelers. A mean-spirited northwesterly *shamal* whipped the community that day, as those blasting windstorms frequently did. Passing by the field, I stopped just beyond right field to watch a couple of innings. Once, as Graham went into his windup, his hat flew into the bleachers; during another windup, the shamal blew *him* completely off the pitching mound. Proof that he wasn't a god. But with the resplendent, square-jawed Dennis Graham on the mound, the Cardinals actually won a few games that year.

Little League enjoyed a special prestige in Dhahran. On each sea-son's opening day—always in April as I recall, with the weather still relatively mild—Aramco provided company flatbed trucks to haul the

Pirates and Steelers around town to the claps and hollers of bystanders as we went by.

For one day, we players felt famous.

FUTURE OIL MINISTER THROWS OUT FIRST BALL

After the (American) national anthem was played at Kings Road Stadium, the Aramco president or chairman of the board or some other dignitary always threw out the first ball—awkwardly, as a rule.

Even the first Saudi president of Aramco and later CEO, Ali Naimi, once threw out the opening pitch; he later became the kingdom's oil minister and chairman of the OPEC.

I remember seeing a wonderful photo of Naimi as a young boy at a special school for Saudi youths Aramco had created in Dhahran in the forties. What caught my eye was the bubbly jauntiness of Naimi, a tiny kid with a big, bright smile, standing with his much taller classmates and teacher. In the picture, he presents a look of easy, casual confidence, a charming cheekiness, that air of unmistakable intelligence that implies, "This kid's going places."

In his hand, he is holding a baseball.

As we players took the field to begin the season-opening game, the atmosphere was always warm and sunny and glorious in our little stadium halfway around the world from the U.S. The home plate umpires who traded off referee duties were Phil Thielhelm and Art Piersol. Every time Piersol made a controversial call, someone in the stands would yell, "Whadaya expect? Piersol only has *one* 'i'!"—meaning "eye."

My first year on the Pirates, we were visited by representatives of our sponsor, Bechtel Builders, a giant global construction outfit that did lots of work for Aramco and probably the Saudi government as well. The reps arrived in shiny suits, looking like chairmen of boards, or *Untouchables* agents. We had a quick photo op, and they left.

We figured we were well-funded.

.333 AND A HOMER

In my final year as a Little League player, three memorable things happened: I batted .333, meaning I got a hit every three times at bat, which isn't bad; I got selected for the league All-Star team, although the champion Falcons nipped us 3-2 in the All-Star game; and I hit my first and only home run ever, a rifle-shot over the centerfield fence that completely startled me.

That homer, as I remember it, was off none other than my pal Beanie Mandis, on the mound for the Steelers that day and a very capable Little League hurler. I sharply regretted it was Beanie who threw that fated pitch and not someone I didn't like; as I rounded the bases in celebration, I noticed he seemed to be trying not to cry while ostensibly smoothing the dirt with his cleats on the pitcher's mound. I felt no joy, only a brief flush of glory earlier as I watched the ball soar over the fence—a splendid moment that vanished as soon as I saw the anguish in my friend's face.

My first-pitch homer with two outs "knotted the score at 2-2," according to the later story in *The Sun & Flare*, but I felt relief when we eventually lost 3-2. Winning, in fact, is *not* "the only thing" as it turns out. Beanie himself hit more than one home run in Little League; in fact, he once hit *two* in *one* game off Abqaiq ace Lexie Smith.

Graciously, Beanie, now grown up and known by the more dignified "Bill," recently emailed me his recollection of my moment of triumph. It happened. But he also remembered a game when he threw pitches that hit four batters in a row.

"I'm pretty sure you were one of them and you actually took one or two steps toward the mound, bat in hand, frown on your face," he recalled, but he does not remember what happened next.

No matter. He says it's still "a day in my life that shall live in infamy," because it cemented his nickname, "Beanie." (When a player is hit by a pitched ball, particularly in the head, he gets "beaned.")

ALL STARS

In 1962 I entered two events in a special competition in tandem with the annual All Star game at champion Ras Tanura's home field: hitting for distance and catcher's throw to second base.

Reasonably speaking, I had no chance of winning either, because RT's Russell Dersch had a far stronger and more accurate throwing arm than I did, and, like a few other players in the league (such as Beanie Mandis), he had *multiple* homers in his stats.

But fate smiled on me that day. As expected, Dersch pounded the ball in the distance-hitting event, walloping it far beyond the outfield fence all over the place, but—a big but—none of these towering drives stayed in fair territory between the foul lines, so they *didn't count*. Astoundingly, not one of the league's top long-ball kings hit a fair ball *over* the fence that day. Neither did I, but I knocked one that *hit* the fence on the fly, and that was good enough to win.

Also, I have no idea why none of the other catchers succeeded in throwing a ball into the fifty-gallon oil drum lying on second base like a canon barrel, its open end facing the thrower. With my relatively feeble arm, I somehow succeeded, by accident, in lofting one ball that eventually rolled into the barrel, which proved good enough to win.

In the end I got two trophies when in a perfectly rational world I should have won none. But, at the time, I was absolutely fine with that.

READING OUR CLIPPINGS

All these little glories were dutifully reported in the *Sun & Flare*, the community's weekly news sheet that was as local as it got. The paper carried Little League box scores and long stories on the heroics of the players. Its articles were big news in Dhahran, or so we kids imagined. We exalted in reading our own press clippings, blissfully unaware that they might reflect a shamelessly exaggerated sense of our actual talents.

SCAVENGER HUNT AT THE CONSULATE

Baseball is only peripherally related to one Little League memory.

It involved a birthday party for a guy on our team named McClellan, a big, barrel-chested, power-hitting kid, whose dad worked at the U.S. Consulate. We were sure Mr. McClellan was a spy. The pale, limestone-block consulate complex nestled in empty, sandy desert near Dhahran Airport, perfectly camouflaged against the pallid surrounding landscape.

McClellan's Mom hosted the party for him and his Pirate teammates at the consulate, and it featured a scavenger hunt, which was new to me at the time. We scoured the desert around the Consulate for items hidden by Mrs. McClellan. For example, our group found one specified item beside a water pump next to the entry gate, another on a window ledge and a third just lying atop the sand somewhere.

The party succeeded wildly—the scavenger hunt was exotic, the hamburgers great, and the chocolate cake indescribably delicious. A perfect trifecta.

CAREER'S END

After I returned to the States, I played American Legion baseball in Arizona for a few years and did well enough that I looked forward to eventually suiting up with my high school team.

But in 1964 tryouts for the McClintock High School freshman baseball team in Tempe, Arizona, fate once again intervened. I pulled my right hamstring beating out a grounder on day two, and during the six weeks it took to heal and without any credentials to hold a spot on the team open for me, an important window of opportunity for my hoped-for high school baseball career slammed shut.

I made the JV team the next year, but having lost momentum and disappointed in my performance, I abandoned the sport and took up basketball, which, it turned out, matched my aptitudes far better.

But I will never forget playing baseball with my buddies in Dhahran in the fifties and early sixties on our vivid-green field of dreams. The memory is indelible, like a fresh, bright chalk line in May from third to home at King's Road Stadium. Like a baseball hit on the sweet spot of your bat, soaring soundlessly far into the brilliant blue sky of a late Saudi spring.

Those were the days.

Me swinging (and missing), 1962. (Courtesy Saudi Aramco)

Me letting someone slide home safe, 1961. (Courtesy Saudi Aramco)

After All-Star game in Ras Tanura.

Little Leaguers get their physicals. (Courtesy Saudi Aramco)

Budding major leaguer. (Courtesy Saudi Aramco)

Little League umpire Piersol.

"Suiting up" the catcher. (Courtesy Saudi Aramco)

Me in the Minor League.

Mike (right) at Half Moon Bay campout.

CHAPTER 27

ON MY HONOR

GROWING UP IN Dhahran, I was trustworthy, loyal, helpful, friendly, courteous, kind, obedient, cheerful, thrifty, brave, clean and reverent.

Except maybe for obedient, thrifty and, almost certainly, brave.

As a Boy Scout, after all, I took our Scout Law seriously. Sort of.

In truth, I joined for the campouts.

FLUBBER PANCAKES

Ultimately, I rose only to the rank of Second Class, one rung above the lowliest, Tenderfoot.

This was due to laziness and lack of disciplined focus necessary to earn any merit badges other than the cooking one awarded for building a roaring fire and burning your food on campouts. And I received that badge despite the pancake batter I once concocted; when rolled into balls and aged overnight, it acquired the consistency of flubber, or "flying rubber," a fictitious material from movie *The Absent-Minded*

Professor, starring Fred MacMurray. My flubber balls would fly a *mile*—roughly—when hit with a frying pan.

Of course, we never actually ate any.

CAMPOUTS

Ah, the campouts.

Mostly, they were long hikes that ended up at Half Moon Bay, a company-managed recreational site popular with Aramcons. A largely unbroken string of one hundred-foot dunes curved along the sandy, crescent-shaped bay, many of them diving almost vertically into the water. When we had campouts there in September, the humidity steamed, and the ground—along with our sleeping bags—squished when we awoke in the morning. Everything smelled dank, of mildew. At sunrise, before we actually did anything, we were pouring sweat as if we'd just run a marathon through a rain forest on a hot day.

Sleeping on dunes presented a challenge. If we laid our sleeping bags on the flat-ish summit at night, we would slowly, imperceptibly creep-slide downward while we dreamed, finding ourselves near its base at sunrise. If the dune had a particularly steep incline, we'd sometimes wake up almost in a standing position a few feet from the bottom. "What the...?"

During the day, we participated in various activities to test our "skills" and instill a competitive but sportsmanlike *esprit de corps.* In one challenge, we had to use compasses to find imaginary objects and to navigate unseen routes to nonexistent destinations. Made sense at the time. Another activity was tug-of-war. Wood chopping for another, with hand axes.

All these endeavors were fine, but dinner offered the most fun because we got to set fires, the overarching goal of every boy under eleven. As we burned our dinners, we also marveled at the beautiful blue bay nearly surrounded by dunes darkening in the setting sun, and campfires flickering like fireflies over the coastal hush. Dinner sometimes reflected the day's competitions, with the winners getting fresh hamburgers and hot dogs to cook, and the losers, canned corned beef hash.

After dinner, stories were usually recited of "physically strong, mentally awake, and morally straight" American supermen and decorated Eagle scouts doing their best for God and country. Sometimes even ghost stories shuddered through the campfire haze.

PROPER KISSING

Just before bedding down about nine, we had free time to "shoot the breeze." At one of these gab fests, an older scout—I think it may have been one of the Johannsens, of which there were about thirty, as I recall—explained to us wide-eyed little boys the mechanics of proper kissing. Where he got such important information and why he felt the need to tell us, we never knew. But it sure *sounded* necessary.

A rumor on one campout—scuttlebutt had it that Girl Scouts were simultaneously camping two dunes over—made the event seem especially promising. Rigorous segregation enforcement meant that, even if they were there, we never saw even one Girl Scout the whole time, although someone in the Wolf Patrol (our troop subdivided into patrols) allegedly sneaked over to the girls' encampment in the dead of night and swiped a pair of underpants from a tent. Oh, sure.

On another campout, something really spectacular happened.

A ROAR IN THE DARK

About midnight, we were slumbering quietly in our bedrolls on the summit of a broad dune overlooking the bay, when we were jolted awake.

Four or five "dune buggies" suddenly and deafeningly roared over the crest of the hill about fifty yards from our encampment, their headlights jerking about in the black night as they bounced down the loose sandbank. Our scout leaders immediately shot out of their tents shouting at the intruders and shining their flashlights in their direction to let them know we were there.

But almost as soon as the *Mad Max* intruders had blasted into our night, they were gone, growling off into the distance, their headlamp beams bouncing crazily down the beach far below. "Who was *that?*" we asked the leaders. "Some stupid guys," the scoutmaster said, annoyed. "Go back to sleep. Show's over."

And that was it.

So, we returned to our sleeping bags, lying on our backs and looking straight up into the glorious sky full of twinkling stars made brighter still by the desert night's dense blackness.

No swimming

You'd think that a campout next to a beach would involve a lot of swimming.

But, no.

For two reasons, swimming was uninviting at Half Moon Bay: 110-degree saltwater and jellyfish the size of catchers' mitts. Both stinging.

So, when we *did* have swimming time, we did not work on our freestyle strokes. Rather, we picked up jellyfish on their non-stinging side and threw them like large Jell-O globs at whoever happened by; our aim, ideally, was for the stinging side to land directly on a target's back as he sprinted desperately away. Should this succeed, you'd feel a little bad, but before long the victim would be launching a blistering counter-attack in which guilt or kindly hesitation could not survive.

The game had karma, I'll give it that. Those gulf jellyfish were particularly disgusting: fleshy, sand-crusty, off-white blobs of indistinct shape, with short, mucous-smeared tentacle globules on the underside like clear caviar.

Ew.

Baby jellies

Years later, I revisited Half Moon Bay as an adult during the annual jellyfish "bloom."

Snorkeling in shallow water, I communed with the hordes of baby jellies floating in like chubby, white, translucent mushrooms rhythmically pulsing their "heads," which all leaned shoreward. Cute little guys from that vantage, even graceful, not the bulbous monsters of my youth.

As the little toddlers approached me, I reached out and bonked them ever so gently on the pillow-tops of their heads, opposite their stingers. They didn't seem to mind, and after a slight pause for their tiny brains to process the interruption, pulsed on.

Night meetings

Being in Boy Scouts felt grown up; the uniforms seemed to promise important if wholly imaginary military action, and my parents had recently started giving me more freedom.

I was allowed to walk the mile or so to night meetings up at King's Road recreation complex, which, considering I was maybe nine or ten, revealed Dhahran's inherent security.

I vividly remember the first time I returned home from a meeting alone. Actually, it unnerved me when I suddenly realized I *was* alone, and that it was black as pitch outside. For long stretches on tree-lined M Street not a creature stirred as I walked briskly, anxiously, on my way home; the street seemed totally abandoned, and the few dim streetlights only embedded thick, deep, ominous shadow along the route.

Somewhere down by the Aramco chairman's house, set back from the roadway by itself, I noticed a tall, lone figure approaching me on the sidewalk, about seventy-five yards distant. It seemed a lifetime before the stranger finally closed the gap, his shadowed adult face appearing dark and dangerous. The balmy night air sent little droplets of sweat slithering down my back. I didn't know this person, which seemed weird; I thought I knew everybody in Dhahran. As he passed by, he briefly glanced at me, expressionless, saying nothing, and I could feel the air move, a bit like when a freight truck passes a small car on a highway. My heart pounded.

Then, nothing.

Fear, I learned that night, can simply be illusion, a reflection of mind and not of reality. I realized the man had just *seemed* threatening. From that point forward, I vowed on my honor to do my best to only be scared of things I actually needed to be scared of.

Right.

Early Dhahran Cut Scout pack. (Courtesy Saudi Aramco)

Scout nears a dune's summit.

Boy Scouts from diverse troops. (Courtesy Saudi Aramco)

Dhahran scouts with Saudi
Bedouin. (Courtesy Saudi Aramco)

Watching scouts clamber up a dune.

'BILLY'

O NE KID IN the neighborhood seemed "different."

At least I thought of him as a kid, though he looked more like a man. All I knew was that he didn't go to school and didn't have a job, which, if a guy didn't do either of those things, I didn't know *what* to think about him.

The kid—let's call him Billy—always seemed slightly dressed up, but I think it was just because, even though he acted like, say, an eight-year-old (which I was), he looked maybe eighteen or thirty-five, and dressed that age. But despite his unusual appearance and a certain blank aspect, Billy possessed what seemed to me like genius in the field of imaginary time- and space-travel.

I spent many hours "traveling" with him through the vast cosmos and human history in a "space ship" someone had built in his yard from old plywood shipping containers. It had pilot and co-pilot "captain chairs," a control console drawn on cardboard, and a bed sheet for the cockpit window, onto which we projected our *Buck Rogers* fantasies.

Sometimes we just used his Dad's car. But whatever the vehicle, we covered a lot of ground—Mars, Venus, the Moon, and even the Wild West and medieval England. Robin Hood to Wyatt Earp to Flash Gordon.

On space flights, we particularly enjoyed the countdown. "... 5-4-3-2-1, *BLASTOFF!*" we'd say in unison. Sometimes we would start out for Mars and end up in Dodge City, Kansas, circa maybe 1876, with Bat Masterson or somebody. Bobby roamed fluidly within his fantasies, and his excitement on these adventures was infectious.

Somehow, I could sense my folks didn't like me playing with Billy, but they didn't stop me, either. Although the other kids in the neighborhood ridiculed him as "weird," he only seemed unusual to me in a good way: He had an unhinged imagination.

When I went into his family's enclosed patio, his mother escorted me to the spaceship, where Billy was invariably already on a journey somewhere. I would sit down next to him, and he'd tell me where we were in the cosmo s—"There's Jupiter!" he would exclaim, turning make-believe dials on the control panel with some urgency. "Put on your seat belt." There was none, so I faked it.

In the end, I drifted away from our astral relationship, probably eventually realizing my interests and capacities were somehow broader than endless fantasy journeys through space-time.

But I think it was important for me to learn that even those of us who seem to have so little to offer can surprise with unique, even astonishing, capabilities. Savants from the outer limits. With Billy, I was often like Calvin's imaginary but sometimes real tiger, Hobbes, in the surreal comic strip *Calvin and Hobbes*, holding onto Calvin's shirttail for dear life as he rocketed off to La La Land on another zany adventure. I believe my abiding fascination with history and the cosmos began in Billy's backyard 'spaceship.'

Frankly, he took me to alien realms I'm certain no one else had ever been before, fueled by a joyous abandon I doubt anyone could ever match.

First Communion (me fourth from right, second row).

CHAPTER 29
JESUS IN ARABIA

I DIDN'T FIND JESUS in Saudi Arabia.

But the idea of him was deeply insinuated in my brain there.

Dhahran perfectly suited Christianity because Americans, virtually all Christian, dominated the camp, and they enjoyed expansive leisure to celebrate their religion, at least behind closed doors. But such stress-free devotion flourished only *within* Aramco communities in the Kingdom; beyond the pale of the community's perimeter fence, apostasy or proselytizing—abandoning Islam or trying to convert Muslims away from their faith, in other words—risked courting the death penalty (for Saudis and foreigners alike).

The authorities uniquely indulged private worship in company camps, where Aramcons of every Christian denomination discretely worshipped at church every Friday, the last day of the Saudi weekend. In Dhahran, church services convened in the theater. Authorities even seemed to turn a blind eye to Christmas lighting displays and the annual live Nativity extravaganza at the ball field, plus a few other American Christian traditions, like Easter egg hunts.

Such religious freedom was prohibited everywhere else in the country beyond Aramco communities, a nod to the company's perceived importance to the Kingdom's hoped-for industrial development and modernization.

Catholicism ostensibly informed the Snedeker family, at least it did for my dad (Mom's bland piety only extended to Christmas and Easter, when hat fashions apparently reigned supreme at Mass; we kids were mainly devoted to fidgeting in church). So, I was "raised Catholic," meaning my parents, priest and lay teachers consistently and persistently indoctrinated me in the sacred stories of that faith from a very young age.

THE COOL MISSIONARY

Occasionally, I even waxed devout in my youth, once very briefly (and foolishly) telling everyone that I planned to become a priest.

This was immediately after hearing a Holy Name Society oration by a young visiting Catholic missionary priest who told manly, exhilarating stories about his exotic experiences in Nepal, where the world's highest mountain—majestic Everest—is located. God is all good and okay, of course, but for a nine-year-old boy, muscle-pumping adventure trumped everything. Somewhere along the way to maturity, though, I lost my religious mojo altogether.

Still, there's a picture I saved of me and thirty or so other kids at our First Communion in Dhahran (It leads this chapter). In the photo, I look positively sainted, my hands pressed together, my eyebrows raised in pious innocence, an aura of otherworldly grace making the image verily glow with imminent salvation. All us kids in the picture look so positively... *clean.*

Today I find that photo simultaneously amusing and slightly terrifying.

SMUGGLING THE BISHOP

The bishop who presided over the Catholic Church's Persian Gulf region, including Saudi Arabia, once visited Dhahran to conduct a confirmation—a church rite of passage for youths into supposed mature devotion. I was one of the novitiates.

The prelate—Bishop Luigi Magliacani (how I actually remember such a tongue-twisting name escapes me)—traveled to us from Rome, the world headquarters of all things Catholic. To us kids, he might as well have been St. Paul. The main thing I remember is having to kiss his enormous, bulbous ring, which everyone else had already slobbered on. This sorely tested my faith.

I had no idea how Aramco imported a Catholic bishop into this very Muslim kingdom in the first place. But old Dhahran pal Beanie Mandis knew, and he clued me in several years ago with this fascinating story:

"My religious dad played a big part in it. He was in [Aramco's] Government Relations Department at that time and had some connections. He helped arrange for the bishop to fly into Bahrain then transfer—to avoid customs—to a *dhow* that sailed for either the Dammam or Khobar pier. His personal interest in arranging this?" Beanie asked rhetorically. "I was one of the confirmation candidates. He didn't tell me about his role in this until later, but I was so proud of him."

ET CUM SPIRITU TUO

Demoralizing and unhygienic incidents aside, spiritual good times occasionally occurred in my childhood as I resolutely absorbed enticements to believe in invisible beings.

Although my family left Dhahran to return to the U.S. "for good" before I became an official altar boy (I was still in training at the time), I learned before we departed to say cool things in Latin, like *et cum spiritu tuo* ("and with your spirit").

Our catechism teacher, Joe Baily, taught us fascinating stories about

St. John Bosco (like the chocolatey syrup), who apparently once dreamed that he came to a high wall and seriously burned his hand when he touched it. Some guy in his dream told St. Bosco that the wall was a thousand miles thick and that a thousand same-sized walls extended beyond it, a thousand miles sandwiched between each, ending at the fiery gates of Hell. The gist of the story, I guessed: Hell is far hotter than we thought. The punchline: When St. Chocolate Sauce awoke, one of his hands was actually *blistered*. Holy smoke.

The physics of this notion can be convincingly disputed, but no matter. St. John Bosco made a profound impression on all of us youngsters, despite scientific questions. Up to then, hell had been a vague threat far too remote for us to actually worry about. After that, it seemed much more immediate.

CHURCH

I barely tolerated mass at the theater every Friday morning, but it did have its charms.

The downward-sloping, amphitheater-style interior contained a wide column of seat rows in the center and two narrower columns on either side (two ample aisles separating them), all flowing like a river down to a raised four-foot-high stage.

Dhahran's Indian Christian domestics employed by local families sat in the side rows *only*; Americans and other Westerners exclusively populated the center column. The crush of Indians on the sides dazzled, their bleached-white shirts radiant as if bathed in black light. The mostly white churchgoers in the center seats, for their part, presented a rainbow of color. The priest and altar seemed extraordinarily high on the stage, pretty close to heaven. Father Roman's short, simple sermons were generally understandable to me each week, because, as I was told later, he wrote them so even an uneducated Indian houseboy with poor English from an impoverished ghetto in New Delhi might comprehend the dogma he sought to convey.

Looking back, I suspect Christian Indian domestics were recruited by the company to work in Aramco camps precisely because they were Christian and more likely than those of other faiths to easily meld with Americans. Recruiting Muslim workers, on the other hand, risked unduly exposing them to Christian influences in a country where leaving their faith would be dangerous.

SMALL WORLD

A religious side note of some interest: In 1990, many years after I first left Saudi and was working as a newspaper copy editor and columnist for the *Rapid City* (South Dakota) *Journal* in the United States, I discovered that my editor-in-chief Joe Karius' uncle and Dhahran's own Father Roman were one and the same. Uncanny.

THE TALL FAMILY

An interesting feature of church in Dhahran was the Benjamins, a family of surprisingly long and lean bodies and faces, as I remember them—two inordinately tall parents and their lengthy, lanky boys.

Somehow, they bring to mind the droll farmer and his daughter in the famous twentieth-century painting *American Gothic*. The Benjamins sat alone in the theater's farthest back-row seats, their backs against the wall, and the two boys—Peter and Michael—always sat slumped far down in their chairs, feet on the back of the seat in front of them. Or so I remember.

Putting feet on seatbacks didn't seem peculiar when *watching movies* at the theater—everybody did it, even after they got scolded by ushers—but it seemed shockingly heretical and gauche when God was *right there* during mass on Friday.

THE BARGERS

Another fun church fact involved Aramco's boyish-looking president, and ultimately chief executive officer and chairman of the board, Tom

Barger, his breathtakingly beautiful wife, Kathleen, and their six children—Annie, Mike, Tim, Mary, Norah, and Teresa.

They presented quite a crew in those days in Dhahran, then a town of mostly young people just starting families. Together the numerous Bargers filled *most of a whole row* in the center column, neat as pins. They were always just a hair late, with practically everyone else seated by the time they sedately single-filed into their row. It always seemed ceremonial to me, like a graduation.

One seemingly out-of-character incident involved an older Barger kid, Michael, probably then an eighth- or ninth-grader. In one of the darker back rows of the theater, those unexposed to light from the projector beam, I spied him during a movie one afternoon *making out* with some girl.

Goodness.

It completely mystified me because I had heard Michael, although spectacularly handsome and obviously coveted by adolescent girls in camp, wanted to become a *priest*. Certainly, even prospective priests weren't allowed to so actively kiss anyone, were they?

In any event, Mike, scarcely alone, had quite a bit of company back in the make-out section. In those clandestine, tantalizing back rows, I learned of some of the wondrous things that surely awaited me when I wasn't a kid anymore.

THE TIE-IN-THE-ZIPPER INCIDENT

Thinking of the theater, I'm reminded of a particularly embarrassing incident one Friday during mass.

Sitting next to my dad one seat from the end of a row, a pretty lady I didn't know slid into the empty last seat, right next to me. Hunched over, bored and vaguely looking at my shoes, I noticed with alarm my fly—the "barn door," as Dad called it—was wide open; a little jolt of electricity shot down my spine.

I figured if I zipped-up really fast, she might never notice, so that's what I did. But because I was all hunched over like Quasimodo, my tie snagged in the zipper. Whoops. I had no choice but to unzip, free the tie, sit up really straight and zip up again, which I did. This subtle ruckus didn't escape Dad's scrutiny, however, and he silently reached over and clamped his thumb and forefinger onto my thigh at that particularly nerve-rich place right above the knee. It was a signal: I had better stop fidgeting or he would *really make me jump around.*

I have no idea if the lady next to me noticed any of this. And I don't want to know.

THE MISSAL MISSILE

In another amusing mass occurrence, one of my altar boy pals—I can't remember which—tripped while carrying the Catholic Bible from one side of the altar to the other.

As the hapless acolyte fell, he flung the sacred book horizontally across the stage—*OH, NO!*—the book and the boy landing with a loud *pow-whomp!* that echoed across the cavernous theater.

I wouldn't have been surprised if a lightning bolt had then shot through the ceiling and fried the whole congregation. But, fortunately, God momentarily spaced out, I guess, and nothing at all happened. Life went on.

HIGH MASS

Some lovely pageantry also occasionally enlivened church services, especially on holy days and particularly at High Masses, which I took to mean Very Very Long and Boring Masses Where the Priest Wears His Fanciest Outfits.

Extraordinary rituals characterized those special observances, some very cool, like the incense-pot rite. The pot, held by the priest and dangled on a long chain, smoldered and smoked with burning incense. Surrounded by altar boys in scarlet robes and lacey white tunics as he moved down the aisles, the priest would swing the pot to and fro, clouds of aromatic smoke wafting about the auditorium like a scene from the caveman movie *Quest for Fire*.

On other special days, Father Roman would sprinkle the congregants with holy water by randomly flicking in every direction a special bottle-like vessel with a perforated spout. The kids strained their heads toward the priest, expectantly, hoping to get hit by some of the droplets and be saved. Or something.

CAMPOUT CHURCH

Religion even followed us on Boy Scout campouts to Half Moon Bay, the Aramco beach recreational area on the Gulf, or into the open desert for a weekend of misery as we learned essential survival skills ("Okay, boys, start your campfires!"), how to walk long, sweaty distances, and the value of ruthless military-style discipline.

Father Roman had to authorize special dispensation for Catholic scouts if they were to miss mass due to a weekend camping trip, but sometimes he petulantly refused. ("What, in God's name, is more important than Mass?!) Even if dispensation *was* approved, the scoutmaster still had to hold little ad hoc worship services—Catholics in one group, assorted Protestants and other apostates in another—next to a sand dune or beach or some such.

We "got" it. God was everywhere, watching, even in the middle of nowhere. Even on weekends.

CALLS TO PRAYER

Overlaying the camp's Christian activities were Islamic exhortations to prayer by *muezzin*, Muslim prayer callers, which wafted sonorously over the landscape several times daily from outside speakers on the Dhahran mosque.

It had to be the only place in Saudi Arabia, as far as I know, where a Christian "church" and mosque co-existed in close proximity, although the "church" was a theater. I loved the sonorous, otherworldly sound of those calls to God, and still do when I hear them, even though I am today resolutely irreligious.

CONFESSION

Religion for me now is like going to confession in the Dhahran of my youth.

In the priest's rectory, a small bedroom served as a confessional. A padded kneeler graced one side of a roughly three-by-five-foot screen with a small mesh window, with the priest sitting on the other side, hidden in shadow. The room was always unnervingly dark when you entered it, before your pupils adjusted.

As I fumbled in the gloom and knelt down to begin, the priest would slide open a little four-inch-square panel, revealing a translucent wire screen lit by a faint glow that seeped into the room from the edges of a closed window shade at the back. "Yes, my son," the voice would say, followed by my part, "Bless me father for I have sinned ..." But the sins I confessed necessarily were arbitrary. Kids, after all, never really do anything all that felonious. That seemed the point, in fact: "they" didn't want you not to know what sins were *exactly* but only to be perpetually terrified of committing any, under the apparent theory that people deathly afraid of sinning would naturally be better people and less inclined toward evil and debauchery. I don't know; the whole charade just made me jumpy.

Whenever I think of religion to this day, I think of that dark, intimidating room, and someone hidden in the shadows who for unfathomable reasons had been granted enormous power over my life. I always wondered why any all-loving divinity would use such fear *in his name* to affect good?

Fortunately, it's a question that seems to answer itself.

My religious views today are symbolized by another confessional, one I once frequented in Tempe, Arizona, in my mid-teens, a normal Catholic church confessional, with two tiny cubbyholes on either side of the priest's enclosed cubicle. Entering one side, garishly lit inside by a single lightbulb, I would kneel down.

The light automatically blinked out.

Heading to Dining Hall after mass.

Santa arrives in Dhahran via camel. *(Courtesy Saudi Aramco)*

C H A P T E R 3 0

CHRISTMAS IN
THE UMMAH

O NE FEATURE THAT made Christmas in Dhahran unique was how Santa Claus arrived.

Sometimes he came alone, by helicopter and without his reindeer (they just wouldn't fit in the chopper, we kids were told). One year a chopper deposited him on the school playground, another time next to the Fiesta Room snack bar. Another year, he rode in on a camel. Sometimes he just appeared in the gym, waiting for kids to arrive.

THE CHRISTMAS LOTTERY

Early in the fifties, because a lot of Stateside amenities weren't yet available in camp or the surrounding Saudi communities, including retail shops to buy Christmas presents, Aramco innovated, as it often did.

The company organized a Christmas lottery, in which, as my mother explained, every mother in camp put a number in a "hat." The lowest numbers drawn got first picks from a mountain of *free* Christmas gifts the company had flown in and piled up in the school gym, the biggest indoor space in town.

But, it was still first-come first-served for all the "winners" when they arrived at the gym to pick out presents opening day. My Mom and other winners spent the night in sleeping bags outside the gym to get first crack at the best stuff in the morning. Once the doors were flung open, Mom said, it was as crazy as a "brassiere sale at Macy's."

Whatever that meant.

CHRISTMAS TREE CIRCLE

During the Christmas season, Dhahran twinkled like a yule tree, including a well-known, twenty-foot-tall hedge trimmed to tree shape in a cul-de-sac off 6th Street.

The dead-end informally but aptly became known as "Christmas Tree Circle," and the tall, conical hedge blazed with lights during the season. In later years, after two Gulf Wars and the Islamic revolution in Iran, the bush was chopped horizontally in half to *not* look tree-like, and its lighting banned.

The revolution and a temporary takeover of the Prophet's Mosque in the holy city of Makkah by Iranians spooked Saudi authorities into accentuating the kingdom's Islamic bona fides and removing any appearances to the contrary. Dhahran's longstanding casual American vibe, where the government seemed to tolerate quaint Yankee cultural customs and religious expression, if discretely entertained, grew far more constricted and restrictive due to new political realities.

NATIVITY—LIVE!

Long before realpolitik rendered Dhahran self-conscious, though, the most glorious of all the community's Christmas observances, by far, was the annual community Nativity pageant, which even venerable *Life* magazine covered in a big pictorial one year.

Even though Dhahran's Nativity didn't include the real Mary and Joseph and infant Jesus, just about everything else seemed mostly genuine. The event incorporated absolutely real bleating goats and baa-ing sheep, and actual, groaning, bad-tempered camels ridden by three simulated but authentic-looking Wise Men in historically convincing outfits. The voice of God in the narration seemed totally realistic, even if it did sound a lot like one of the teachers we all knew at the school.

The pageant graced the expansive, grassy outfield of King's Road Stadium. Aramco workmen erected a mini-Bethlehem and manger as historically faithful as possible, and an exceedingly tall tower rose majestically high over the tennis courts, the North Star perched atop with sacred singularity. We spectators jammed the bleachers along the first-base line, bundled up and shivering against the chilly winter wind that invariably wafted in from the desert beyond once the sun set, our clapping muffled by our woolen mittens.

As a kid, my friend Beanie Mandis got cast in the pageant one year, and he recalls a skittering Keystone Cops Moment:

"The Nativity was always directed by a woman named Ivee Fullerton who, I believe, was the head secretary at the front desk at the school," Beanie wrote to me in an email. "One year I was cast in the show as 'third Shepherd Boy.' My role was to capture the baby goat from the flock and deliver it to Joseph in the manger. The goat was uncooperative, and the sizable audience cracked up as I chased him all over the field trying to catch him, falling down several times as I slipped on goat shit. I finally gave up, pretended to pick up and hold an invisible baby goat, and delivered him to Joseph, who, God bless him, bailed me out by playing along with the pantomime."

Half the townspeople were acting as characters in the pageant, but the stands still were invariably full. It was always an unfailingly beautiful *Silent Night*, the North Star shining brightly in the dark heavens, the shepherds and Wise Men ecstatic at finding the newborn Messiah in a lowly Bethlehem stable bathed in soft Aramco-donated electric light, and the omnipotent bass voice of the Creator booming authoritatively through the night air.

Perfect.

What Aramcon—heathen and hosanna singer alike—could even *think* of missing it?

POST-NATIVITY

Over the years, as I noted earlier, Dhahran's demographic complexion transformed dramatically. It gradually evolved from being an almost wholly American, Christian-majority place into a demographically complex, cosmopolitan community.

Today, its roughly twelve thousand residents represent some seventy different nationalities, Americans now but a tiny minority, perhaps only a few hundred souls. The town's demographics somewhat track those of the company as a whole, in which Saudis in 2016 comprised more than eighty-five percent of Saudi Aramco's 65,282 employees, and the remainder made up of non-Saudi Arabs from such countries as Lebanon and Egypt; Filipinos, Pakistanis, and Indians; and a few Westerners, such as Americans, Brits (and other Europeans), Australians and a smattering of other nationalities.

Muslims are now the majority in Dhahran, a demographic shift that profoundly altered the community's heretofore casual tolerance of public Nativity performances and other non-Muslim public religious expression, although discrete *private* observances still occur unmolested behind closed doors.

But, in the Age of Eisenhower, with the local Nativity extravaganza a widely anticipated annual event, free presents distributed to kids and festive Christmas lighting glowing throughout the community, Christmas grandly arrived in Dhahran and the other Aramco camps in the midst of arid, alien desert. It had been a unique historical moment, when quasi-colonial outposts of low-key American economic imperialism were able to enjoy a vibrant Christian holiday season in the heart of the *Ummah*, the global Muslim community.

It was a lovely time, and the Saudis we knew were very gracious and accommodating about the idea of Christmas when they visited camp in December, as we were toward the annual Islamic holy month of Ramadan and the *Hajj* pilgrimage to Mecca (events that, due to the Islamic lunar calendar, methodically moved a few days through our Gregorian datebook each year).

Sadly, the warm ambience of religious tolerance prevailing then has grown faint over the ensuing years amid the ever-more-militant fear and loathing of extremism in the Mideast.

I will always remember those halcyon days fondly as a priceless gift of the gods of fortune, and the spirit of Saudi forbearance past.

Dhahran's iconic Christmas Tree Circle. (Courtesy Saudi Aramco)

Decorating for Christmas. (Courtesy Saudi Aramco)

Extras prepare for Dhahran Nativity.

Nativity presentation at ball field.

Saudi Aramco headquarters area, Dhahran today. (Courtesy Saudi Aramco)

CHAPTER 31

POSTSCRIPT

A T THE BEGINNING of the sixties as it neared the time my family would leave Dhahran behind for good, I couldn't wait.

Only eleven at the time, I had already been in the Kingdom nine years. I felt bored with the place and ready for new horizons.

As we finally lifted off from Dhahran Airport in the early summer of 1962, with the powerful engines of the commercial jetliner roaring, I was glad to leave the utterly familiar for the largely unknown in Tempe, Arizona, where a new house awaited in a new suburban development. Unfortunately, my dad hadn't done his homework thoroughly, so he didn't know that the housing subdivision we were moving to would prove inconveniently far from the schools we would attend, and everything else for that matter.

Oh, and the U.S. economy sucked at the time.

RECESSION

A recession then gripped America, and age discrimination in employment remained legal and rampant in 1962.

My fourty-two-year-old father faced help-wanted ads—pitifully few to begin with—that prohibited anyone over thirty-five from even applying. His cold calls to companies in the Phoenix area met wariness because of his age and his salary in Dhahran, which had been somewhat higher than stateside (potential employers fretted that, if they hired him, he would leave as soon as he found a better-paying position elsewhere).

So, he ended up investing much of his savings in a new company that ostensibly created algae products for the space program but actually fronted a fraud run by a charlatan, who soaked up savings of unsuspecting investors (including other ex-Aramcons) to fund his luxurious, criminal lifestyle. The company quickly tanked, and its devastated victims didn't have enough money to pursue justice in the courts. Investors, then, were reduced to trying to scrape by as best they could, including my dad and, by extension, us.

Everybody in our family got jobs late that demoralizing winter—after Dad somehow made sure we kids had presents and a beautiful Christmas, his favorite holiday.

In January I started picking up baseballs at the local Luke Appling Batting Range in the Salt River's dry floodplain, and mowing lawns, while Kathy babysat and Mike bagged groceries at a local supermarket. After much bowing and scraping, Dad eventually secured a manager's job at Motorola, then a growing semiconductor manufacturer, and Mom—who had barely ever worked in her adult life—went to work on a Motorola assembly line.

We survived our fallen fortunes and, after a long while, even thrived. The experience proved, as Dad always promised, a "character building" exercise that taught all of us the "value of a dollar" and the intimate connection between personal labor and success.

Those facts on the ground in our brave new world in America profoundly shaped my subsequent life into adulthood. Despite intermittent struggles over the years, fate proved not only charitable but generous.

For some reason, and I've heard this innumerable times from other

Aramco "Brats," I could never seem to *fully* leave Dhahran. It followed me wherever I went in my life, like an advertising jingle you can't get out of your head—"Double your pleasure, double your fun ..."

To this day, Brats from eras throughout Aramco history keep in touch and share the secret handshake of the experience: a unique suite of memories and experiences. A Brat website, including a chat group, used to exist but apparently is now for sale, while regular and irregular reunions are still held around the country. I rarely go, because I'm just not that sociable, but I completely understand the pull to share long-ago memories of our lives in that dusty, magical camp in the desert. Non-Brats never seem to get it. The Dhahran experience is an alien, over-wrought thing to them.

But to us Brats, it's as clear as the pale-blue Saudi sky in July, clouds as white as fresh whipped cream, and an alarming heat that makes your skin instantly tighten.

It never leaves us. As we say, "You can never get the sand out of your shoes."

Deja vu

When I first returned to Saudi Arabia as an adult, 20 years after I left as a kid in 1962, it seemed surreal, because everything in Dhahran appeared almost *exactly* the same as it had when I departed.

The wide, lushly landscaped streets looked the same, though the trees were of course much larger. The homes looked the same, if freshly painted and re-roofed. The school looked the same, as did the baseball field down the hill, although a soccer/track complex had been added and some other recreation amenities. The Dining Hall, Bowling Alley, Theater, Commissary, Community Library and old Aramco administration building were all still existent and in great shape, but several modern new admin towers had been added in the company's "Core Area," where the business end of Aramco—now Saudi-owned and renamed Saudi Aramco—towered over the community.

The King's Road Stadium field of dreams also was still extant, green as the hills of Africa. But more than twenty years later it would be torn down to create a huge, grassy commons for the growing community. Nothing lasts forever, even a field of dreams.

To recapture my youth and bask in *déjà vu*, on my first day back in the summer of 1982 I immediately drove around the community. The gate guards, surprisingly, had waved me perfunctorily through. I drove by all the old haunts, including Christmas Tree Circle, whose conical hedge by then had been chopped horizontally in half but with its hidey-hole at the base still intact where the older kids used to smoke and "make out."

I easily found our old house, 4491-B, looking almost eerily the same, as though I'd just taken a short stroll around the block rather than just returned from a twenty-year exile.

Later, I discovered—much to my astonishment—that some of the old childhood gang I hung out with were still in Dhahran, working for Aramco and living in camp with their wives and kids instead of playing guns in the old neighborhood off 8th and M streets. Old Dhahran Pirates teammate Bill Cohea still lived in town, as burly as ever, as did Beanie Mandis and Bill Scott, of the arch-rival Dhahran Steelers. Adult Beanie looked identical to his childhood doppelganger but bigger, while Bill Scott, who seemed prematurely big and muscular in Little League, apparently hadn't grown much since.

It was fabulous seeing these guys again, and they were graciously welcoming, but it became quickly and unsurprisingly (if disappointingly) evident that, by leaving Dhahran at eleven—and completely missing the boarding-school and returning-student experiences—I had also missed the years critical to cementing the deep and lasting fellowship that longtime friends develop. We Brats from different eras had naturally drifted into alien realms over the years with our far different experiences, and whereas we all shared memories of a Dhahran childhood, theirs contained far more years, complexity and richness than mine. To my old childhood friends, I sensed I represented mostly a dim, distant recollection in a lifelong continuum of expatriate experience. One tiny ping in millions of remembrances.

But for me, most of my boyhood seems crammed exclusively into those nine Dhahran years, undiluted by the memories of future shared experience with the same kids as we grew older. I was necessarily an outsider in that context. But a kindly regarded one.

So, Beanie and Bill and Chris and Kay and Linda and Algie and Wadia and Saib and Pamela and all the others, in one sense, will always be kids under eleven to me, part of an eternally innocent and poignant childhood that I will always treasure. Those playmates from Dhahran long ago populate my memories of the community to this day, as though they are forever young, although I know some have already left us for the great hereafter.

Why should I still be so entranced by remembrance of such a sandy, hot, isolated island of existence so many years ago? The environment was one of a kind, certainly, but we didn't really know that at the time. It was just home.

I think my fond recollection is due to Dhahran's enveloping ease and safety. Growing up there I never wanted for anything it seems and had reason to fear little. Everybody had moms and dads and sometimes even grandparents in the house; certainly, no poverty existed within camp (and we didn't recognize its symptoms beyond the fence); and kids had tons of constructive diversion in the community and lots of adult support to grow and develop. Getting into real trouble proved difficult at best. And you got to travel the world.

What was not to like?

INDIFFERENT AMERICA

However, the experience did set me apart, not necessarily in positive ways.

When I returned to the U.S., many of my references when talking to people were foreign and probably sounded elite and arrogant. But that's all I knew—"When I was in Hong Kong ..." And my formative experiences were shared by few people, except Brats. Yet my youth in Dhahran also broadened my horizons, taught me that America wasn't the be-all, end-all of existence. That the world is almost unknowably large and complex.

Ironically, growing up in the semi-utopia of Dhahran taught me to question *everything*, especially the traditionally embraced but unsubstantiated ideas that dominate modern life, like religious faith and "American exceptionalism." The expat experience continues to help me untangle the thickets of ignorance and misunderstanding and aggressiveness I encounter in American culture as elsewhere, although I often find myself alone in pushing back against what seems like dangerous nonsense. But, what I learned in the nurturing comforts of Dhahran long ago gives me hope that things aren't hopeless.

And it left a beautiful archive of memories to enjoy until I ride off on a figurative camel into the sunset.

It turns out, I was never bored in Dhahran. I was mistaken.

CHAPTER 32

THE VIDEO

DECADES AFTER I left Arabia as an eleven-year-old boy, I came across a random walk-around video of Dhahran shot in 1996 by a Brat named Rodney Burge.

In the middle of the video, Burge arbitrarily walked down M Street, turned onto 5th and then veered eastward onto a familiar-looking concrete walkway. He passed by one duplex and opened a tall gate into the large "front" yard of an apparently vacant house next door. He peered in the undraped windows at the empty, silent living room, the kitchen, the bedrooms.

I suspect Rodney's purpose with the film was to provide a sense of déjà vu to Brats who might view it, to show the places we might fondly recall in the community, to show how many familiar Dhahran icons from our childhoods had barely changed over long decades.

He continued through the side yard of the home, to the "back" yard and then into the alley, turning around to face the duplex, still filming. On the tree next door, I read this on the address plaque: 4491-A. Our next-door neighbor.

This meant Burge had been walking through the yard of our old house—4491-B—and was now standing directly in front of the Snedeker home's entry from the alleyway. The alleyway where most of my exceptional, exotic, very good childhood had played out.

Still filming, he opened the gate and inadvertently re-entered my past.

The End

ABOUT THE AUTHOR

AFTER LIVING TWENTY-SEVEN years on and off in Saudi Arabia, one of the hottest places on the planet, Rick Snedeker retired and left the desert kingdom in 2011, relocating to South Dakota, one of the coldest. Happily, sheltering inside during the icy assault of Great Plains winters, he finds plenty of time to write.

A former newspaper and magazine journalist and public relations editor, Snedeker has written, in addition to this memoir, a nonfiction manuscript—*Holy Smoke: How Jesus Conquered America. How It Might Be Liberated*—about how Christianity became deeply embedded in America and persistently perpetuates. He also writes a personal blog called *Godzooks,* (The Faith in Facts Blog), published on Patheos Nonreligious, the world's largest hub for non-theist bloggers. He writes op-ed pieces for assorted newspapers and magazines as well.

CPSIA information can be obtained
at www.ICGtesting.com
Printed in the USA
LVHW080817080620
657648LV00019B/1604